ARCHITECTURAL SKETCHES
&
FLOWER DRAWINGS
BY
CHARLES RENNIE
MACKINTOSH

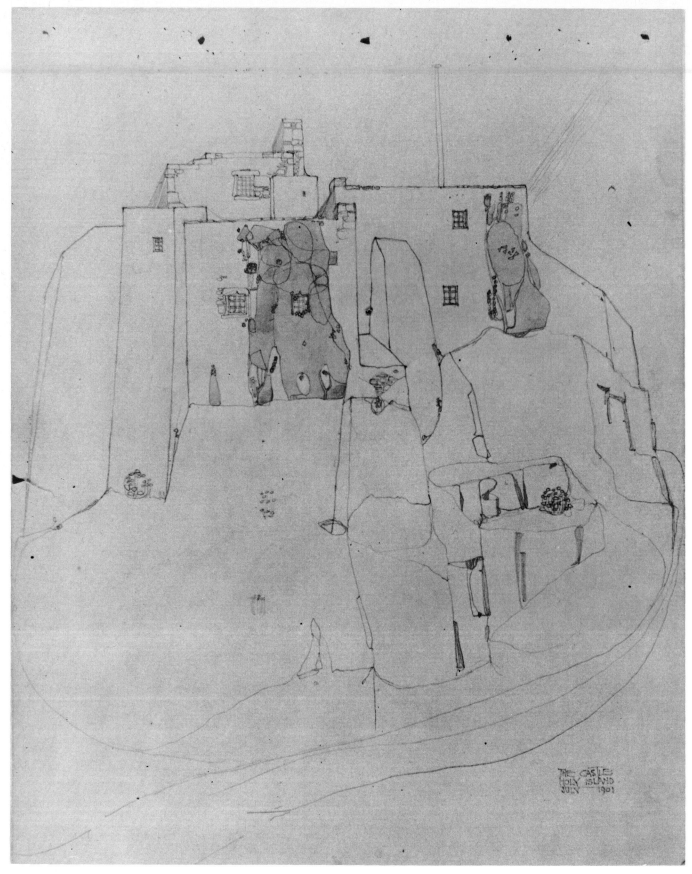

The Castle, Holy Island, 1901 260 × 203 GU

ARCHITECTURAL SKETCHES
&
FLOWER DRAWINGS
BY
CHARLES RENNIE
MACKINTOSH

Roger Billcliffe

Assistant Keeper, University of Glasgow Art Collection

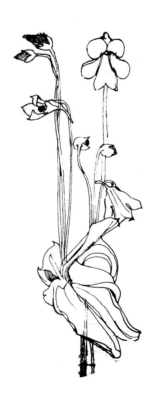

ACADEMY EDITIONS·LONDON

ACKNOWLEDGEMENTS

My thanks are due to the University of Glasgow and the Glasgow School of Art, particularly its Director, H. Jefferson Barnes, for permission to reproduce works from their collections; to Robert Cowper, Grace Watson and William Leitch of the Photographic Unit at the University of Glasgow, who produced all the photographs used in this book; and to Margaret Miller and June Barrie for deciphering and typing my manuscript. I would also like to thank Ruari McLean for his considerable help.

For Bron and Owen

First published in Great Britain in 1977 by
Academy Editions 7 Holland Street London W8

SBN Cloth 85670 315 X   SBN Paper 85670 149 1

Printed and bound in Great Britain by
Balding & Mansell Ltd., Wisbech

CONTENTS

LIST OF ILLUSTRATIONS

BLACK AND WHITE

BLACK AND WHITE

All measurements are in millimetres, height before width.

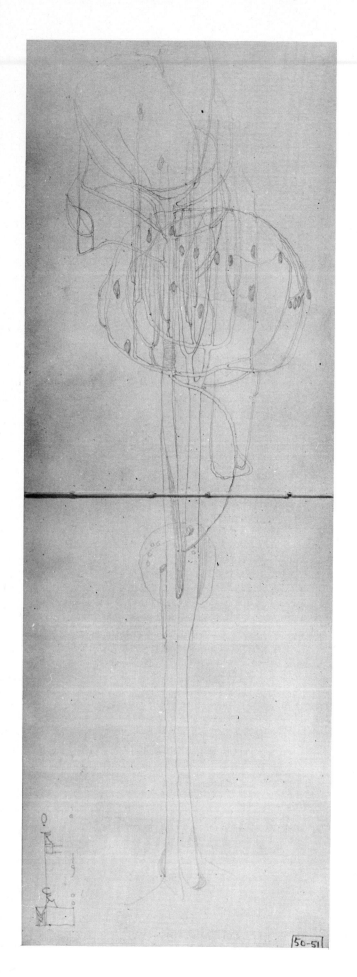

Tree, 1900 370 × 134 GU
A very stylised drawing, and possibly the earliest to have the joint initials of Mackintosh and Margaret Macdonald. (They were married in 1900.)

INTRODUCTION

An architect's sketchbooks will probably give the historian a far greater insight into his design processes than many of his finished drawings for specific buildings. The sketchbook enables one to experiment, to play around with composition, plan, elevation or sections, to concentrate on specific features or ornament, even to doodle; it will remain a record of, hopefully, private thoughts, and need have none of the deliberation or precision of measured drawing. Such sketchbooks will probably have a dual purpose – that of 'thinking aloud' while developing some new project, along with that of recording things seen, some striking detail drawn both for its own sake and its possible future usefulness. Perhaps the camera has replaced this latter function, perhaps architecture today does not draw so heavily on details of earlier buildings – whatever the reason, few architects' sketchbooks of today will be so revealing to the historians of tomorrow as those of Charles Rennie Mackintosh.

Everywhere Mackintosh went he took his sketchbooks; it was a habit he retained from his youth to his fifties, some years after he had given up the practice of architecture. He used his sketchbooks to record what he saw and what interested him, not just buildings but furniture, inn signs, lamp-posts, railings, even gravestones. The same books were used year after year, and were filled up with working details, doodles, notes, extracts from train timetables, and even used as diaries. Above all they were working books. The drawings were intended to be used, and features from English cottages will appear translated into Scottish villas and public buildings: to Mackintosh his sketchbooks were reference books, to be thumbed through for a particular detail, whether for a building or a piece of furniture, an endless source of inspiration. But they were also scrap-books, family albums, lasting memories of family holidays, where all of the group had their initials recorded on the drawing.

Over the years the content of the books gradually changed, and the style of drawing with it; the later sketches of Kent and Sussex are conceived as finished drawings, often with watercolour additions. Mackintosh also used watercolour in what may be the earliest of his sketchbooks, used for scale drawings, perhaps a student's notebook (page 19). The early drawing of Rowallan Castle (page 19) has a similar tightness, but the watercolour of Spynie (page 26) begins to reflect some of the new skills he was acquiring from his studies at the Glasgow School of Art. The Italian tour sketchbook of 1891 sets the standard for his sketches for the next ten years. In his diary[1] of this tour he records the places he visited, the time he spent sketching and his comments on the buildings and objects he drew: 'S. Jerome, [Verona], very beautiful example of Italian Gothic brick and stone work' (page 20); 'Como Cathedral very good . . . Trancepts [sic] and chancel very good Renaissance Work' (page 29); 'S. Maria del Grazie [Milan] . . . has a very good Renaissance

porch' (page 9). Some of the drawings were sent back to Glasgow for the annual School of Art Club exhibition. Mackintosh was awarded first prize, and one of the judges, Sir James Guthrie, told the School's director, Fra Newbery, that their author should be an artist, not an architect.[2] In fact for the next few years, much of Mackintosh's output was in the form of paintings, and not buildings. As a junior draughtsman in the firm of Honeyman and Keppie his work was probably routine, leaving him with

Porch, S. Maria delle Grazie, Milan, 1891 231 × 162 GSA
On a later page in this sketchbook are some sketches of details at the Glasgow Art Club, for which Honeyman and Keppie were commissioned to design new interiors in 1893. Mackintosh was responsible for much of this work and based his designs for the vestibule on this porch.

time to produce the watercolours and drawings, for the School of Art Magazine for instance, that have come to be known as the Glasgow Style. With Herbert MacNair (1868–1955) and Frances (1874–1921) and Margaret (1865–1933) Macdonald he formed a group known as 'The Four', whose distinctive style of draughtsmanship and eerie symbolism permeated the School and influenced many other students.

Mackintosh never forgot that he was an architect, however, and even his beautiful Italian drawings were pressed into service as inspiration for details of Glasgow's buildings. The porch of S. Maria delle Grazie was translated into the Glasgow Art Club, ostensibly designed by John Keppie, but much of the detail being worked out by Mackintosh. In a lecture, *Architecture*,[3] read to the Glasgow Institute of Architects in February, 1893, Mackintosh displayed his knowledge of the writings of W. R. Lethaby, particularly his *Architecture, Mysticism and Myth* published the previous year. Mackintosh found in Lethaby the confirmation of many of his own evolving beliefs – that architecture was the synthesis of all the fine and applied arts, that a new mode of expression must be found for modern buildings. 'Old architecture lived because it had a purpose. Modern architecture, to be real, must not be a mere envelope without contents'.

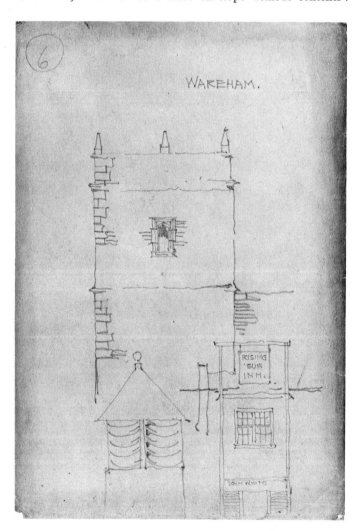

Holy Trinity Church and the Rising Sun Inn, Wareham, 1895
181 × 127 GU
An unusual juxtaposition, but Mackintosh certainly remembered this drawing, as it forms the inspiration for his design for the inn at Lennoxtown, September, 1895.

Lethaby praised the sense and order of old buildings; the appropriate form and materials for the requisite function were a natural progression from this, and Mackintosh began to study the vernacular architecture of earlier ages. The early issues of *The Studio* in 1893, with the articles illustrating Voysey's work would have reinforced these views; Mackintosh's reaction to these new influences are shown in his 1894 sketchbook.

There are no sketchbooks to record Mackintosh's visits for the years 1892–93; but in 1894 he went to the island of Bute, and then spent some days in England. His later sketchbooks show that he followed this pattern in other years, spending his main holiday in England or abroad, and making only a few drawings of Scottish subjects. This does not mean that he was not aware of nor interested in Scottish vernacular architecture. It may be that other sketchbooks, now missing, were filled with Scottish buildings, but a more likely answer is that through the five volumes by D. McGibbon and T. Ross, *The Castellated and Domestic Architecture of Scotland* (1887–92) Mackintosh had all the source material he needed. The subject matter hardly ever changes in his sketchbooks, either, although the way it is drawn certainly does. The buildings which attracted him are all of the traditional vernacular style that so much inspired Lethaby. Mackintosh was interested in small houses, inns, barns, manor houses and small castles; parish churches occasionally attract his attention, cathedrals very rarely, and modern buildings (i.e. post 1850) never. Yet Mackintosh as an architect was no historicist. Punctiliousness and absolute accuracy in the use of historical detail was not his way; he can be said to be striving to achieve a free style of architecture, having affinities with the past but not dependent upon it. The historical vocabulary he used in his buildings came partly from his sketchbooks, and to help create his free style he deliberately sought out a specific type of building.

The majority of buildings Mackintosh drew in the mid to late 1890s had had their style dictated, not so much by fashion, as by use and tradition. They were not individual like the great houses and cathedrals, they were generic and their style non-specific. It is only with the help of the sketchbooks that we can say that the inn at Lennoxtown[4] is derived from the Rising Sun Inn at Wareham (page 10); that bay windows in the main entrance at the Glasgow School of Art are inspired by those in houses at Lyme Regis (page 44) or Chipping Campden (page 32), that the staircase towers at Scotland Street School certainly owe something to Falkland Palace (pages 59 and 64). Mackintosh chose, therefore, to record buildings whose features would be incorporated in his own work, without prejudicing or dominating the style he wished to create. It was not idle fancy or speculation which inspired Mackintosh to draw certain buildings. The number of specific references to the sketchbooks in his designs are too numerous for them to be dismissed as coincidence. I think one can say that the sketches were made methodically, in that Mackintosh was determined to use certain features in his own work, as opposed to saying that the drawings were made for their own sake and that a later usage of them was coincidental.

This theory perhaps makes Mackintosh out to be a far more methodical and rational person than has often been suggested. This can be supported in a number of ways. The sketchbooks contain no drawings of modern buildings, but David Walker[5] has conclusively shown how aware Mackintosh was of work produced in the 1880s and 1890s, especially, in England. Much of this work was illustrated in the architectural magazines of the period, and if one makes an analogy with the sketchbooks, then Mackintosh will probably have indexed articles which particularly appealed to him. His 1893 lecture showed he was already aware of men like Belcher, Shaw, Bentley, Bodley, Stokes and Sedding, names which he said would probably be unknown to his audience of Glasgow architects. But Mackintosh knew them, although his knowledge is patently second-hand, in that he was not aware that the works by Belcher which he admired were almost certainly controlled by his assistant, Beresford Pite. We also know that Mackintosh was systematic enough to keep, not only his sketchbooks, but several hundred drawings, photographs, diaries, account books, letters and journals (now mostly in the collection of the University of Glasgow) until his death; this was long after the immediate relevance of most of the items had passed, but still he kept them and even transported them all to London with him when he left Glasgow.

We know that Mackintosh was constantly using his old sketchbooks. Drawings on adjacent pages may be separated by over ten years in date. Nor were the sketchbooks only brought out for his sketching trips, as details of tearoom furniture, Miss Cranston's house, Hous'hill, and Bassett-Lowke's house appear between the drawings of flowers and English houses. The sketchbooks, therefore, were consistently referred to in the drawing office, so the holiday sketches would be constantly in his mind.

Although Mackintosh consciously sought out his subject matter, with the intention of compiling his own reference books, this does not mean that the drawings are at all dry or mechanical. Despite their deliberate purpose, there is no doubt that they stand up for themselves as works of art.

The drawings are each minor masterpieces. They are assured and elegant, and Mackintosh uses the shape of the page and the versatility of his pencil to their utmost. He must have worked at amazing speed, sometimes producing several carefully worked-out drawings in a single day. There is no hesitation, no rubbing out of mistakes – if there are any they are cleverly incorporated into the design. A whole page might be given to a detail of a lamp, a weather vane, an iron railing or a tracery window; and on the opposite page is a wide-sweeping view of a village street, or the rising masses of Holy Island, an elevation of the keep of a castle or a church tower, all with the same essential detail recording just what he needed to know to use in his own work. Most exquisite of all are the flower drawings. Flowers fascinated Mackintosh, and he made drawings of them all his life. Delicately coloured with simple washes, or just soft pencil drawings, they capture the beauty and delicacy of flowers and explain their shape and structure without the mesmerising detail of more usual botanical illustrations.

The drawings tell one a lot about the personality of Mackintosh. It is not difficult to see that spelling was not one of his virtues. The manuscripts of his lectures are littered with such mistakes, and the silent 'k' makes rare appearances on his drawings. Proper names, too, defeated him, Chipping Campden and botanical names giving him particular trouble. But this does not matter greatly, as the drawings tell us far more about the positive side of Mackintosh's character. The same attention to detail that is so characteristic of his decorative schemes is just as apparent in these sketches. Every detail on a flower seems to be there, every pane of glass in a window, every tile and board. Mackintosh obviously took pleasure from making the sketches, and the detail is there for its own sake as much as any other purpose.

In some of the drawings there appears a clue as to the sources of many of his early watercolours for *The Magazine*.[6] The weird symbolism and semi-architectural structure of many of these watercolours is difficult to decipher. Similar patterns and structures are occasionally found in the sketchbook, where Mackintosh incorporates two drawings on one page, often at right angles to each other and with some degree of overlapping. In other pages a section of a door jamb might appear alongside its elevation or plan, and occasionally these separate facets of information are overlaid to create a complex pattern. The drawings of St. Cuthbert's, Holy Island (page 65), with their superimposed flowers are examples of the first type, as is the Saxlingham drawing of 1905 (page 64) which is further complicated by the similarity in appearance between the shape of the door latch and the barn itself. Some drawings are far more complicated, however, and the drawings of the kitchen range in a cottage on Holy Island, 1906 (page 73) appear almost undecipherable at first glance; on this sheet many different pieces of information have been recorded in the form of plan, section and elevation, each overlapping another; not haphazardly, however, for Mackintosh seems to have been attempting to impose some overall conception of design or pattern on the page. This is more

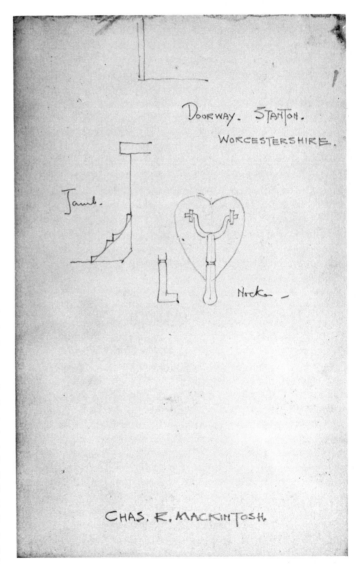

Door knocker, Stanton, 1894 178 × 116 GU
Metalwork details, like handles and knockers, were a favourite theme, although the spelling of 'knocker' defeated Mackintosh on this occasion.

apparent, and more successful in the Cintra drawings of 1908 (pages 74, 77 and 78).

A gradual change appears in Mackintosh's sketchbook drawings about 1900. He no longer seems to be searching for individual detail in the buildings he sketches, and he also tends to use a larger format of sketchbook. The Falkland Palace drawings (pages 59 and 64) are perhaps the earliest examples of these full page drawings of buildings seen from a distance, with more emphasis on the picturesque and romantic qualities of the subject. The style is confirmed at Holy Island in 1901 (frontispiece, 68, 69, 70 and 71) and thereafter the earlier type of sketch almost disappears. There seems to be no clear reason for this change of style, but a number of other features appear in his work at the same time. Colour appears for the first time since his Italian tour, in the form of a watercolour wash about 1900; there is a greater number of flower drawings; his output of sketches decreases, and there is none of the sense of speed or urgency about the Holy Island drawings that there is about those of Broadway, Lyme Regis, Wareham or Norfolk of the later 1890s.

There are a variety of factors which could possibly have caused this change in style and one of the most important of them is Mackintosh's increasing maturity. Not only do his sketches change around 1900, so does his architecture. There is a sense of restlessness or experiment that is difficult to define about the Art School, Queens Cross Church, Ruchill Street Halls and the three early buildings, Martyrs Public School, Queen Margaret Medical College and the Glasgow Herald Building. Even the furniture and decorations for Miss Cranston's Tearooms at Buchanan Street and Argyle Street are perhaps a little brash or crude, and at the same time hesitant. Windyhill spans this phase and the next, the assured design of The Hill House, Scotland Street School and the second phase of the School of Art. The assurance and refinement of these later works is echoed in the drawings. Whereas the 1890s work, in both sketchbooks and buildings, is a period of intense search for a new vocabulary and a working out of new ideas, the next decade is calmer as Mackintosh resolves his problems and his style. He is only topping up his reference books, and can afford to pay more attention to the object itself.

There is a widely held view that Mackintosh's marriage to Margaret Macdonald in 1900 was behind many of the apparent changes in his work. A charge often levied against her is that she diluted his work, made it more frivolous and feminine by the incorporation of her own designs in his. Without doubt, Margaret played a greater part in Mackintosh's interior design schemes and furniture design after 1900, but I think it was at his invitation and not her insistence. Holders of the opposite view point to the appearance of her initials on the Holy Island and later drawings, believing them to indicate that she added the colour washes. Nothing could be further from the truth, and there is a simple explanation for the changes. Although Mackintosh and Margaret met about 1893, it is very doubtful that they would go on holiday together before they were married – society, and the Macdonald family, would not have approved. Margaret's initials certainly do not appear on any pre-1900 drawing, and indeed, Mackintosh did not always sign them himself. When her initials do appear on a drawing, they are always in Mackintosh's handwriting, not hers, so she did not put them there herself. If her initials are there because she applied the colour wash, what is the explanation when there is no colour wash? And what is the explanation when five initials appear on a drawing? The answer is a simple one. Mackintosh

began to treat these drawings as more permanent memories of holidays taken by him and his wife, and his family. He adopted the habit of recording the initials of the people who were at his side whenever he made a drawing and as he rarely went anywhere without Margaret, her initials appeared with his. He rarely, if ever, allowed her to add to his drawings, nor did he amend hers, and the watercolour washes are all his. If further evidence is required to refute the legend then a flower drawing of 1901,[7] bearing the initials MTFBC, surely provides it: the initials stand for Margaret (M), Mackintosh or Tosh (T), Frances (F), Herbert MacNair or Bertie (B) and Charles Macdonald (C), the brother of Margaret and Frances. Surely all five did not produce the drawing!

Marriage to Margaret did have its effect upon Mackintosh, and his changed life style with more relaxed family holidays probably gave him the time to produce these more coherent drawings, but other changes in his life probably had an influence upon his change of subject matter. Mackintosh went through a number of crises after 1905, and his changed attitude towards architecture is reflected in the sketchbooks. More and more drawings of flowers were made, and the tranquility of the drawings is in direct conflict with what happened to Mackintosh after 1910–11. Again the insinuations that Mackintosh ran out of ideas, took to drink, made enemies of his few clients are at most a simplification, and at worst a deliberate and sustained attack on his character. That he made enemies there is no doubt. They were fellow architects in Glasgow, jealous of his success and acclaim in Europe. Whatever the causes for his actions in 1911–13, the vicious stories of a cantankerous and drunken old man are grossly exaggerated, often by those who had much to gain by his leaving Glasgow (nor could he be considered old – he was 45 when he left Glasgow). Whatever the causes of these changes they are mirrored in his sketchbooks – in 1900 and in 1913 – by the changing subject matter.

When he left Glasgow he settled at Walberswick and was later invited to go to Austria. In 1914, letters in German to an odd character who spent his time sketching on the dunes of Suffolk caused local suspicions. His accent did not help him, and he was arrested by the Suffolk police as a spy; he probably had as much difficulty understanding them as they did him. Eventually, he was released, but left Suffolk and its wild flowers and moved to London. There he failed to set up a new architectural practice, and determined to start a new career as an artist.

He died in 1928, having spent the previous years painting watercolours in the hope of having an exhibition in a London gallery. The sources of these watercolours are undoubtedly the post-1900 drawings, and the delicately coloured flower drawings. His subject matter is the townscape and landscape of the south of France, not the Northumberland and Kent villages. But the same flair and assurance are there, with the one major difference that they are for public consumption and not private contemplation. They are no less revealing, however, of Mackintosh's spiritual and physical well-being, than the hasty yet delicate Italian sketches were of his enthusiasm and purposefulness, thirty years earlier. Mackintosh was a natural and prolific draughtsman, but each drawing has its purpose and each tells us a little more about the enigmatic personality of its creator.

NOTES

1. Coll. University of Glasgow Art Collections
2. Howarth, p. 11
3. Coll. University of Glasgow Art Collections
4. McLaren Young, no. 112
5. David Walker *Charles Rennie Mackintosh* in *The Architectural Review*, September, 1968
6. Coll. Glasgow School of Art
7. McLaren Young, no. 288

BIBLIOGRAPHY & ABBREVIATIONS

Howarth:	Thomas Howarth, *Charles Rennie Mackintosh and the Modern Movement*, 1952
McLaren Young:	*Charles Rennie Mackintosh*, introduction, notes and catalogue to Edinburgh Festival Exhibition by Andrew McLaren Young, 1968
Macleod:	Robert Macleod, *Charles Rennie Mackintosh*, 1968
Walker:	David Walker, *Charles Rennie Mackintosh* in *The Architectural Review*, September, 1968
Jottings:	*Architectural Jottings by Charles Rennie Mackintosh*, selected by Andrew McLaren Young, 1965
GU:	University of Glasgow Art Collections
GSA:	Glasgow School of Art

CHRONOLOGY

VISITS	LIFE
1868	Born, June 7, Glasgow.
1884	Began professional training with John Hutchison, Glasgow, and commenced classes at Glasgow School of Art.
1886	Sketches of Old College, Glasgow	
1887	Sketches of Glasgow Cathedral	Awarded two prizes by Glasgow Institute of Architects.
1889	Elgin Cathedral Rowallan Castle Spynie Castle	Joined Honeyman and Keppie, Glasgow, where he met Herbert MacNair (1868–1955). Awarded one of Queen's Prizes, South Kensington, for design of a Presbyterian Church.
1890	Sketches of Glasgow Cathedral	Awarded Alexander Thomson Scholarship for design of a public hall. Awarded National Silver Medal, South Kensington, for design of a museum of science and art.
1891	Italy: Naples, Palermo, Rome, Orvieto, Siena, Florence, Pisa, Pistoia, Bologna, Ravenna, Venice, Padua, Vicenza, Verona, Mantua, Cremona, Brescia, Bergamo, Lake Como, Milan, Pavia; return via Paris and Antwerp	A paper on *Scottish Baronial Architecture* read to the Glasgow Architectural Association.
1892		Designs for a chapter house for Soane Medallion Competition; awarded National Gold Medal, South Kensington, for this design. A paper *Italy*, read to Glasgow Architectural Association.
1893	Sketches at Lamlash, Arran	Glasgow Herald Building designed. Project for a railway terminus for Soane Medallion Competition. A paper, *Architecture*, read to Glasgow Institute of Architects.
1894	Langside, Stirling and Ascog, Bute, Broadway. Buckland, Willersey, Winchcombe, Evesham, Stanton and Chipping Campden	Queen Margaret's Medical College, Glasgow.
1895	Langside, Maybole, Crosraguel, Baltersan Castle, and Corrie, Arran, Bridport, Lyme Regis, Merriott, Whitchurch Canonicorum, Abbotsbury, Christchurch, Wimborne Minster, Wareham, Burton Broadstock, Puncknowle, Montacute, Studland, Symondsbury, Chideock and Misterton	Martyrs Public School, Glasgow. Interiors at Gladsmuir, Kilmacolm.
1896	Langside and Prestwick Orkney	Glasgow School of Art Competition. Stencil decorations at Buchanan Street Tearooms, Glasgow.
1897	Blythbury, Halesworth, Norwich, Framlingham, Cawston, Westwick, Moreton, Wrexham, Bramfield, Wangford, Reydon, Tuggleshall, South Cove,	Queens Cross Church, Glasgow, designed. Furniture designed for Argyle Street Tearooms, Glasgow. Building begins at Glasgow School of Art.

	VISITS	LIFE
	North Elmham, Swanton Abbot, Wenhaston, Walsingham, Sall and Worstead	
1898	Tavistock, Ashburton, Stoke Gabriel and Exeter	Project for Glasgow International Exhibition, 1901. Ruchill St. Church Halls, Glasgow, designed. Gravestone designed at Kilmacolm.
1899		East wing of Glasgow School of Art completed. Westdel, Glasgow decorations and furniture. Windyhill, Kilmacolm, designed. Interiors and furniture designed at Dunglass Castle, Dunbartonshire. Frances Macdonald and Herbert MacNair married.
1900	?Falkland Palace, Fife	Interiors and furniture at Ingram Street Tearooms, Glasgow. Interiors and furniture at own home, 120 Mains Street, Glasgow. Interiors and furniture at 34 Kingsborough Gardens, Glasgow. Work exhibited at Vienna Secession. Married Margaret Macdonald.
1901	Holy Island ? York	Windyhill completed. Further rooms at Ingram Street Tearooms. Daily Record Office, Glasgow, designed. Stands designed for Glasgow International Exhibition. Designs for 'Haus eines Kunstfreundes' competition. Gate Lodge, Auchenbothie, Kilmacolm, designed.
1902		Exhibited at Turin. Hill House, Helensburgh, designed. Liverpool Cathedral competition drawings. Wärndorfer Music Salon, Vienna, designed.
1903		Interiors and furniture for Hous'hill, Nitshill, commenced. Design work for Willow Tearooms, Glasgow, commenced.
1904	Scilly Isles	Willow Tearooms opened. Mackintosh becomes partner in the firm. Scotland Street School, Glasgow, designed. Furnishings designed for Holy Trinity Church, Bridge of Allan.
1905	Saxlingham, Stopham, Cley, Blakeney	Furniture designed for Hous'hill and Windyhill. Fireplace designed for Miss Rowat, Paisley. Gravestone at East Wemyss, Fife.
1906	Holy Island, Bowling	Moved house to 78 Southpark Avenue, Glasgow. Commenced design for west wing of Glasgow School of Art; Mosside, Kilmacolm; Auchenibert, Killearn; and rooms at Argyle Street and Ingram Street Tearooms.
1907		Building of west wing of Glasgow School of Art commenced.
1908	Cintra, Portugal	Interior work at the Lady Artists Club, Blythswood Square,

VISITS		LIFE
		Glasgow.
1909	Blairgowrie, Withyham, Groombridge	West wing of Glasgow School of Art completed. Fireplace, furniture and decoration for Hous'hill.
1910	Chiddingstone, Hever, Leigh, Penshurst, ? Cowden	
1911		Cloister Room and Chinese Room at Ingram Street Tearooms. Gravestone for Talwin Morris. Restaurant for Miss Cranston at 1911 Glasgow International Exhibition.
1912	Bowling	
1913	Holy Island	Alterations at Mosside, Kilmacolm. Left Honeyman and Keppie.
1914	Walberswick	Left Glasgow and moved first to Walberswick.
1915	Walberswick	Moved to Chelsea. Designed conversion of a terrace house in Northampton for W. J. Bassett-Lowke, 78 Derngate.
1916		78 Derngate completed. Fabric designs for Messrs. Foxton and Messrs. Sefton, London.
1917		Designed 'The Dugout' for the basement of the Willow Tearooms. Furniture for Bassett-Lowke and F. Jones, Northampton.
1918		Furniture for Bassett-Lowke.
1919	Buxted	Cottage at East Grinstead for E. O. Hoppé. Memorial fireplace for 'The Dugout'.
1920	Worth Matravers	Design for studios, studio flats for the Arts League of Service and a theatre for Margaret Morris.
1921		Book covers for Blackie & Sons.
1923	Port Vendres	Settled in South of France.
1924	Amélie-les-Bains	
1925	Mont Louis	
1927		Returned to London.
1928		Mackintosh died of cancer of the tongue.
1933		Margaret Macdonald died. Memorial Exhibition organised in Glasgow.

THE PLATES

S. Agostino, Milan, 1891 231 × 162 GSA

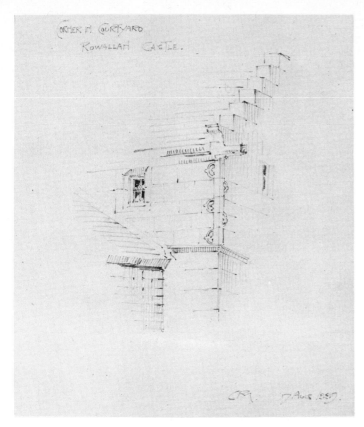

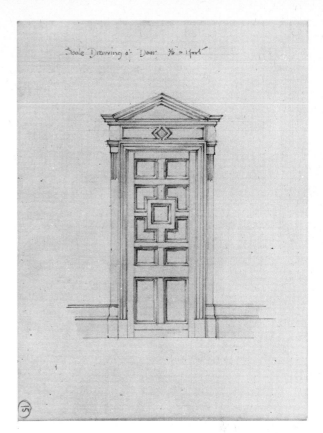

Detail of a corner gable in Rowallan Castle, 1887/9 260 × 171 GU
Some other very mechanical drawings, similar to this, were made
of Glasgow Cathedral in 1887.
The date on this drawing is ambiguous, and could be 1887 or 1889.

Scale drawing of a door, c.1886–7 182 × 134 GU
Mackintosh's earliest remaining sketchbook is full of
architectural details and this is perhaps part of the work
for which he won a prize from the Glasgow Institute of
Architects in 1887.

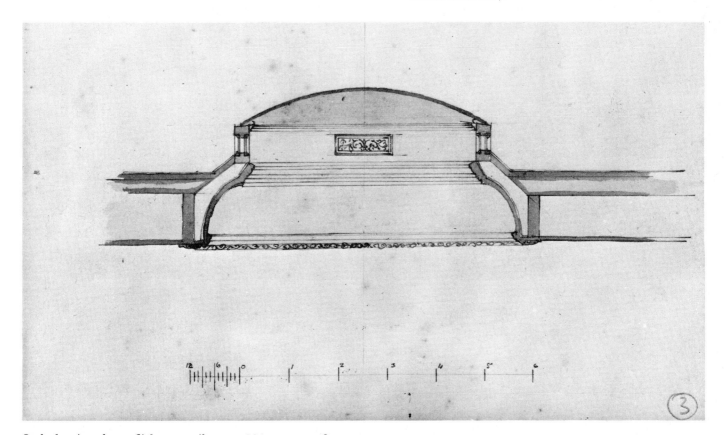

Scale drawing of a rooflight or ventilator, c.1886–7 134 × 182 GU

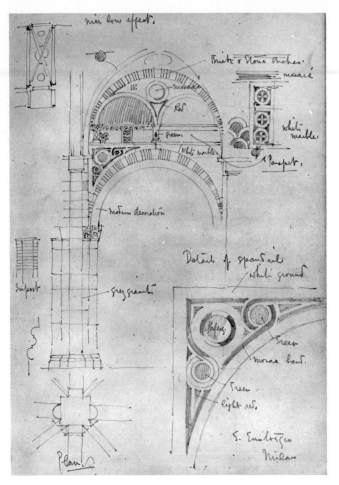

nice low effect.

Brick & Stone Arches.

mosaic

White marble

Parapet.

mosaic

W.

Red.

Green.

White marble.

modern decoration

Impost

grey granite

Detail of spandril
white ground

Perfect

Green

mosaic band.

Green.

light red.

S. Eustorgio
Milan

Plan.

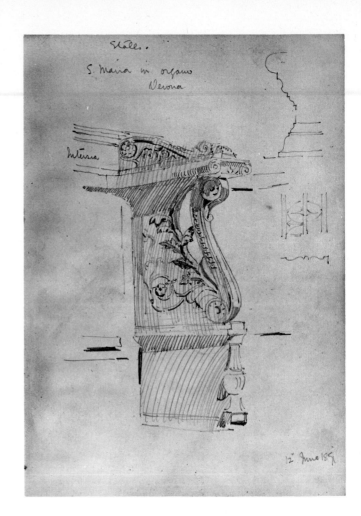

Stalls.

S. Maria in organo
Verona

Interior

12ᵗʰ June 1859

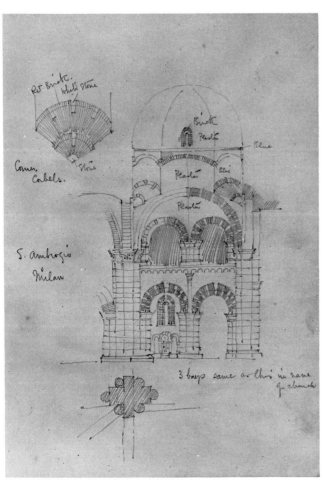

Red Brick.
White stone.

Corner Corbels.

Stone

Brick
Plaster

Blue

Plaster

Blue

Plaster

Plaster

S. Ambrogio
Milan

3 bays same as this in nave
of church

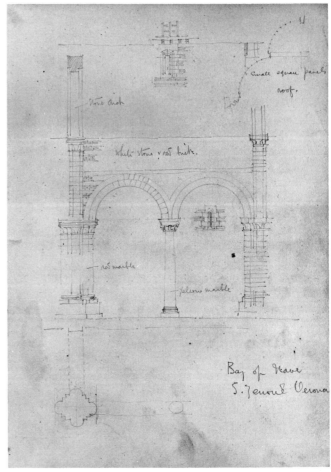

small square panels
roof.

Stone Arch

White stone & red brick.

red marble

Veronese marble

Bay of nave
S. Zenone Verona

Flower drawing, 1901 185 × 134 GU

Opposite

TOP LEFT
S. Eustorgio, Milan, 1891 231 × 162 GSA

TOP RIGHT
Choir stalls, S. Maria in Orgamo, Verona, 1891 231 × 162 GSA
Mackintosh's sketchbook for the latter part of his Italian tour,
starting in Verona on June 12th, 1891, fortunately survives. It
shows how his drawing style has matured; it is less hesistant and
mechanical than the Scottish drawings of the 1880s, but still does
not yet have the fluidity of the Somerset drawings of 1894.

BOTTOM LEFT
S. Ambrogio, Milan, 1891 231 × 162 GSA

BOTTOM RIGHT
Bay of the nave, S. Jerome, Verona, 1891 231 × 162 GSA

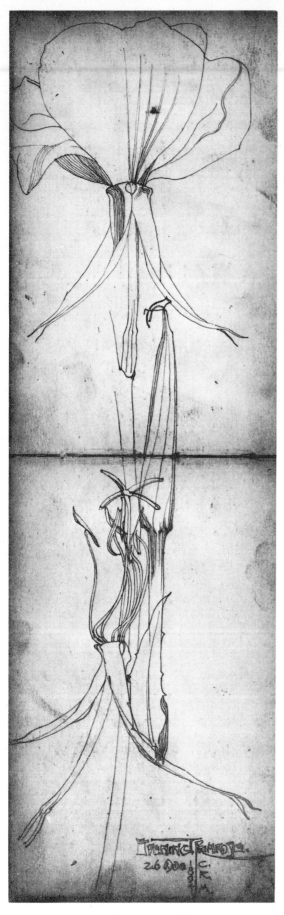

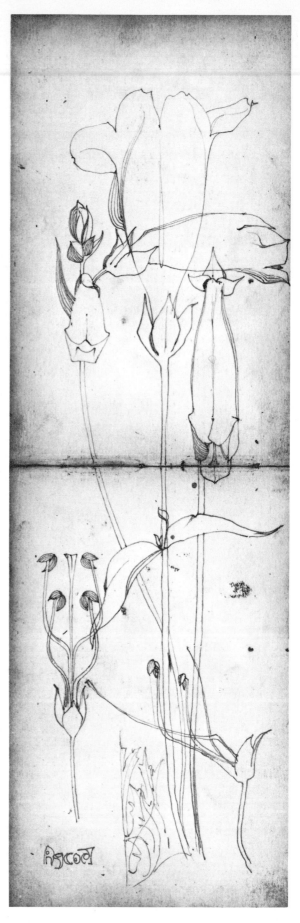

Evening primrose, Ascog, Bute, 1894 352 × 115 GU

Antirrhinum, Ascog, Bute, 1894 352 × 115 GU
Mackintosh's early flower drawings are all in pencil without any watercolour addition.

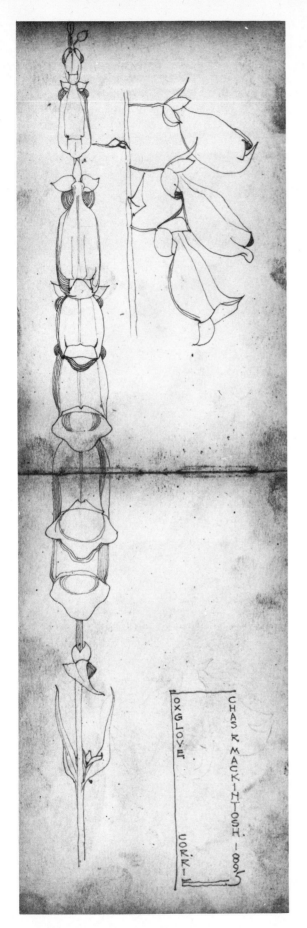

Foxglove, Corrie, Arran, 1895 352 × 115 GU
This rendering of the foxglove flowers in dead elevation recalls some of the details on Mackintosh's posters of this date. Just as the details of the Lyme Regis cottages were absorbed into the design for the School of Art, Mackintosh even made use of his flower drawings.

Pinguicula – bog violet, Corrie, Arran, 1895
352 × 115 GU

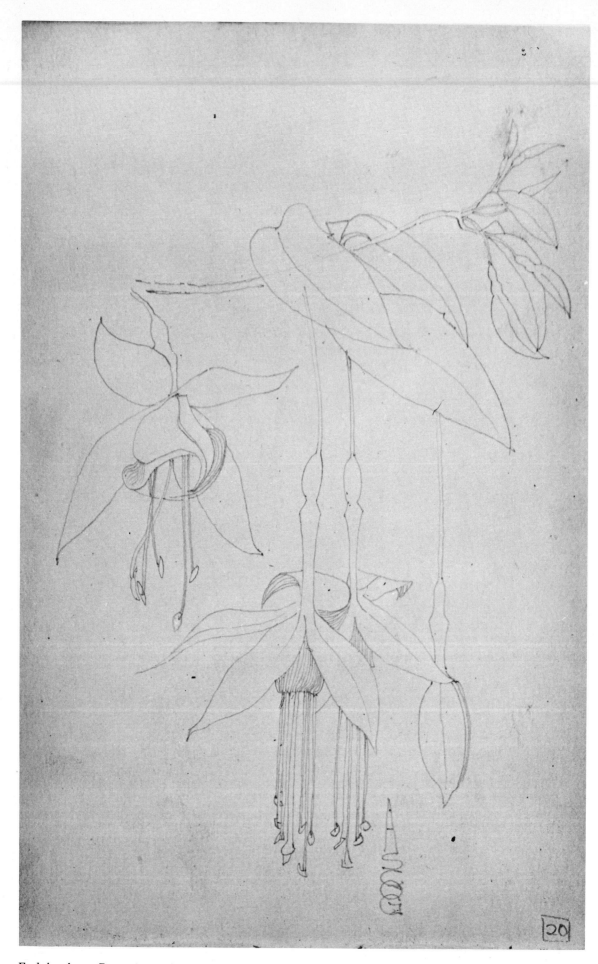

Fuchsia, Ascog, Bute, 1894 176 × 115 GU

La Rue du Soleil, 1926–7 Watercolour 407 × 393 GU

In 1921 Mackintosh, after a series of battles with officialdom over his designs for studios in Chelsea, gave up architecture and decided to devote himself to painting. In 1923 he moved to Port Vendres on the Mediterranean coast of France and began work on a series of watercolours, which occupied him until his death in 1928. The Dorset work of 1920 can be seen as transitional between this series and the early sketches. Although there is the same keen observation of detail, it is here recorded for its pictorial and compositional value, not as part of an architectural vocabulary. Pattern and colour dominate the series, and few of them surpass this drawing of the reflection of the village in its harbour: the detail of foreground and distance are rendered equally and the shimmer of the moving water and the geometrical shapes of the buildings combine to give the drawing an almost abstract appearance.

Oasthouses, Chiddingstone, 1910 180 × 228 GU
The sketches of this period are more finished, and a number like
this one are worked up into watercolours; it is no longer some
specific historical or structural detail which interests Mackintosh.

Window, Spynie, Morayshire, 1889 254 × 175 GU
Mackintosh was in Elgin in 1889, and this drawing
was probably made on the same tour.

Glasgow Cathedral at sunset, 1890 394 × 283 GU
The signature shows the original form of his name;
it became *Mackintosh* about 1892/3. A more artistic
view of the cathedral than his earlier drawings of it,
which are similar to that of Rowallan Castle.

The Downs, Worth Matravers, 1920 Watercolour 450 × 537 GSA

The Village, Worth Matravers, 1920 Watercolour 445 × 545 GSA

In July, 1920 Mackintosh revisited Dorset with his wife and their friends from London, Randolph Schwabe and his family. The more pictorial style of the earlier Kent and Walberswick sketches has here been taken up in earnest, and Mackintosh is drawing purely as an artist, rather than observing his subject as an architect. He has not completely forgotten his training however, as there is a strong formal, even structural pattern in these 1920 water-colours, which is developed further in his French work.

Rosemary, Walberswick, 1915 269 × 204 GU

Veronica, Walberswick, 1915 276 × 209 GU

Pine cones, Mont Louis, 1925 262 × 206 GU
The Mackintoshes stayed at Mont Louis in the Pyrenees, before finally settling in Port Vendres, on the French side of the Franco-Spanish border. This is the latest known flower sketch by Mackintosh, who was by this time working hard on his series of landscape and flower paintings.

Como
Cathedral.

Ref.

Details of Como Cathedral, 1891 231 × 162 GSA

The Turret House, Stirling, c.1894 176 × 115 GU

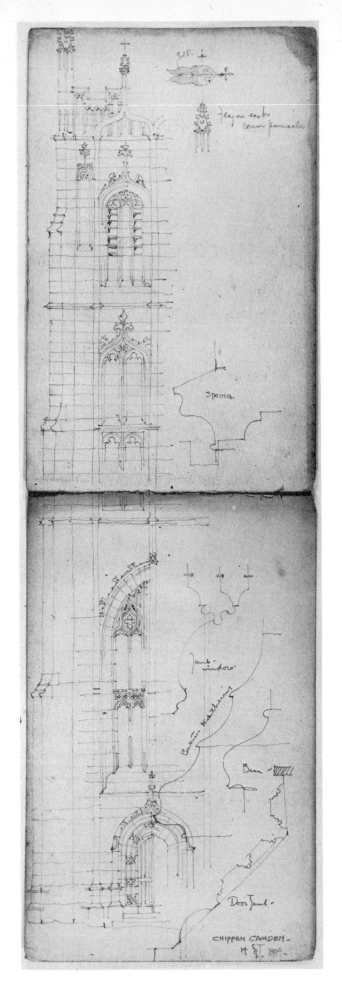

Chipping Campden Church, 1894 178 × 115 GU

Chipping Campden Church, 1894 352 × 115 GU
Compare this with the adjacent illustration to see Mackintosh's differing attitudes to the same subject. This drawing is in dead elevation, spreading over two pages of his sketchbook, with details and sections of jambs and buttresses; the other drawing is more freely executed, the church being viewed from an angle and very little detail being recorded in the drawing.

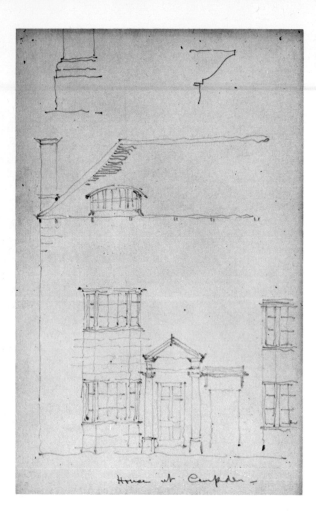

House at Chipping Campden, 1894 178 × 116 GU
The double height bay window was to be used by Mackintosh in
his design for the entrance bay at the Glasgow School of Art.

House at Broadway, 1894 116 × 178 GU

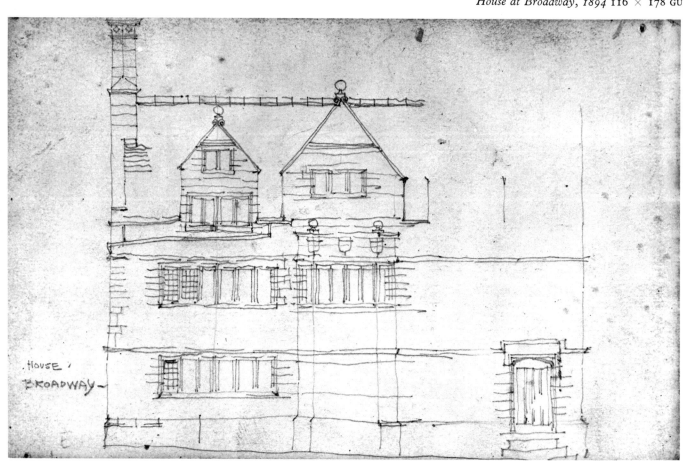

House at Buckland, 1894 116 × 178 GU

Old Alms House, Broadway, 1894 116 × 178 GU

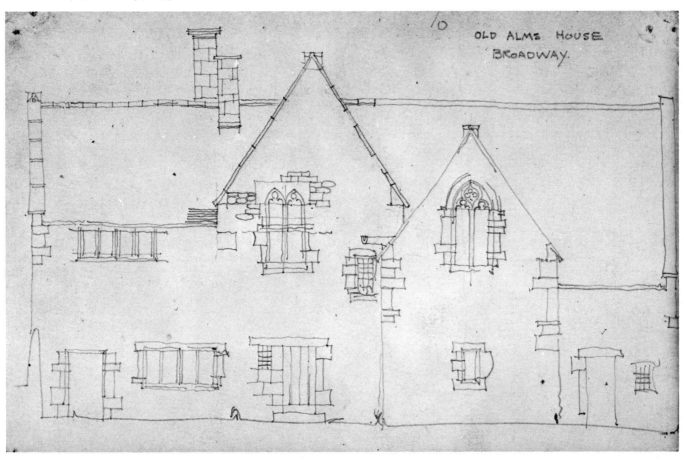

Detail of a door, 1894 178 × 116 GU

Wrought iron gate, Evesham, 1894 178 × 116 GU

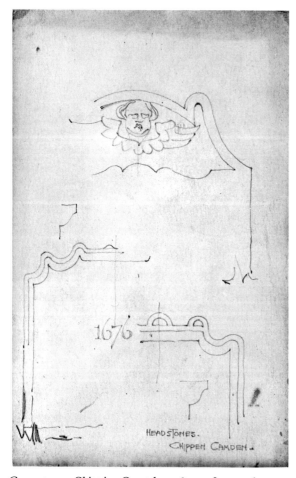

Gravestones, Chipping Campden, 1894 178 × 116 GU

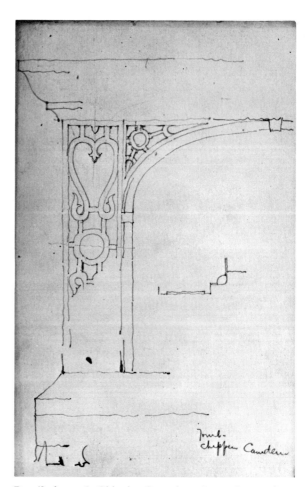

Detail of a tomb, Chipping Campden, 1894 178 × 116 GU

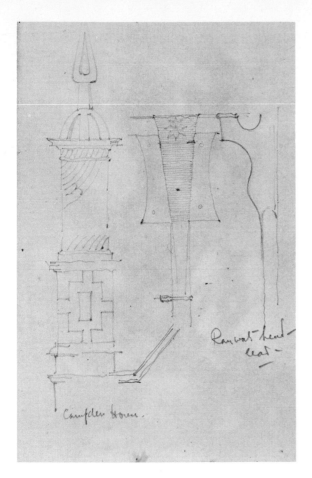

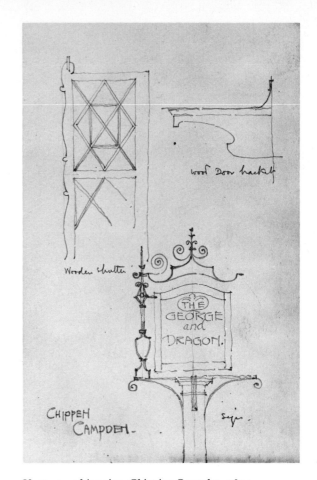

Pinnacle and rainwater head, Campden House, Chipping Campden, 1894 178 × 116 GU
Mackintosh made particularly skilful use of rainwater pipes in his buildings, especially at the Glasgow Herald, and the Glasgow School of Art.

Shutters and inn sign, Chipping Campden, 1894 178 × 116 GU

Door architrave and inn sign, Broadway, 1894
178 × 116 GU
In September, 1894, Mackintosh toured the area around the borders of Worcestershire and Gloucestershire, where he virtually filled a sketchbook with drawings of churches and traditional English buildings.

35

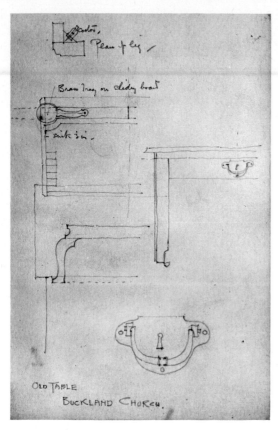

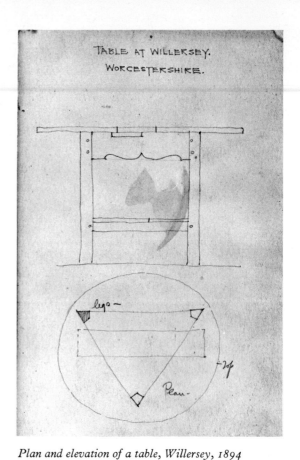

Details of an old table, Buckland Church, 1894
178 × 116 GU
Very similar handles to these were designed by
Mackintosh for his early pieces of furniture for
Guthrie and Wells, c.1894–5.

Plan and elevation of a table, Willersey, 1894
178 × 116 GU
Mackintosh developed a similar combination of
circular top over three legs in his tearoom furniture
of the later 1890s.

Iron railings at Chipping Campden Church, Worces-
tershire, 1894 178 × 116 GU

Details of oak panels, Broadway Church, 1894
178 × 116 GU

Spurge, Withyham, 1909 258 × 202 GU

Sea pink, Holy Island, 1901 258 × 202 GU
An early coloured flower drawing.

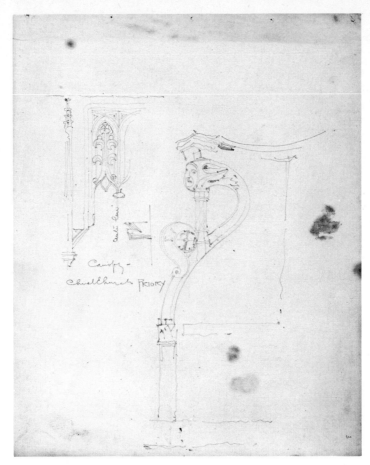

Details of choir stalls, Christchurch Priory, 1895 260 × 205 GU

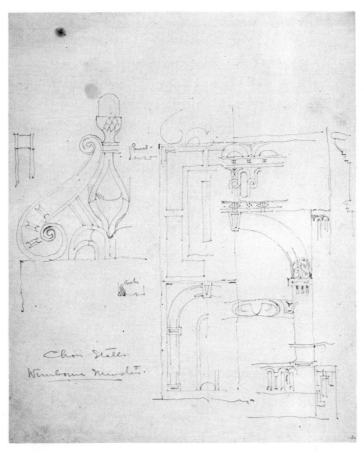

Choir stalls, Wimborne Minster, 1895 260 × 205 GU

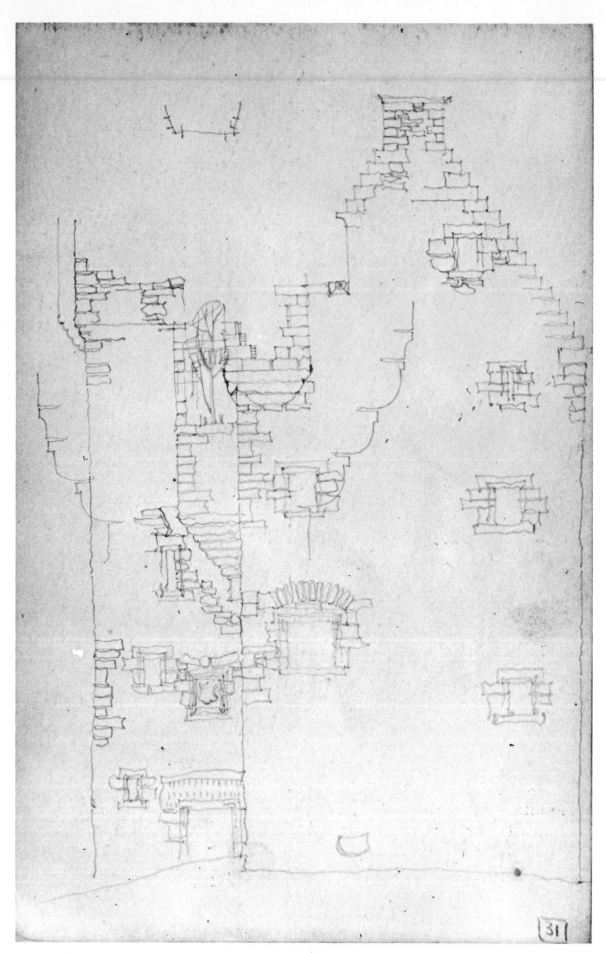

31

Baltersan Castle, Ayrshire, 1895 176 × 115 GU
The traditional crow-stepped gables and dressed stone door and
window openings attract Mackintosh again.

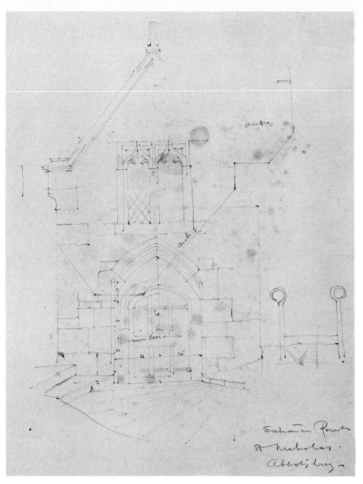

Entrance porch, St. Nicholas, Abbotsbury, 1895
260 × 205 GU

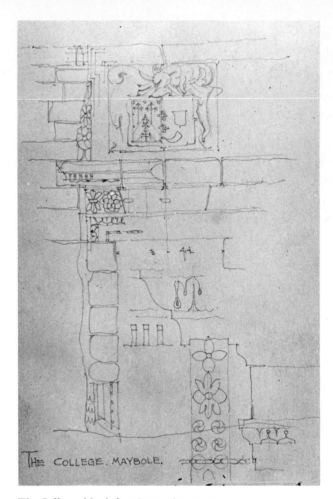

The College, Maybole, 1895 176 × 115 GU

House at Broadway, 1894 178 × 116 GU

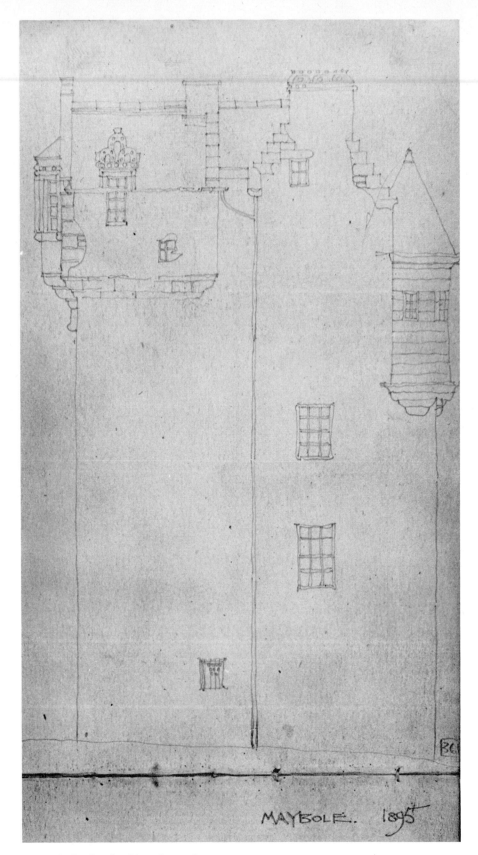

Maybole Castle, Ayrshire, 1895 176 × 115 GU
Features from Maybole Castle (which were, however, to be found in many other Scottish tower houses of the period) re-appear in the east elevation of the Glasgow School of Art, for instance, the corbelled-out oriel window and the apparently random composition of roof lines and windows. The device of running a rain-water gutter through a dormer window was used at Windyhill, Kilmacolm, 1899–1900.

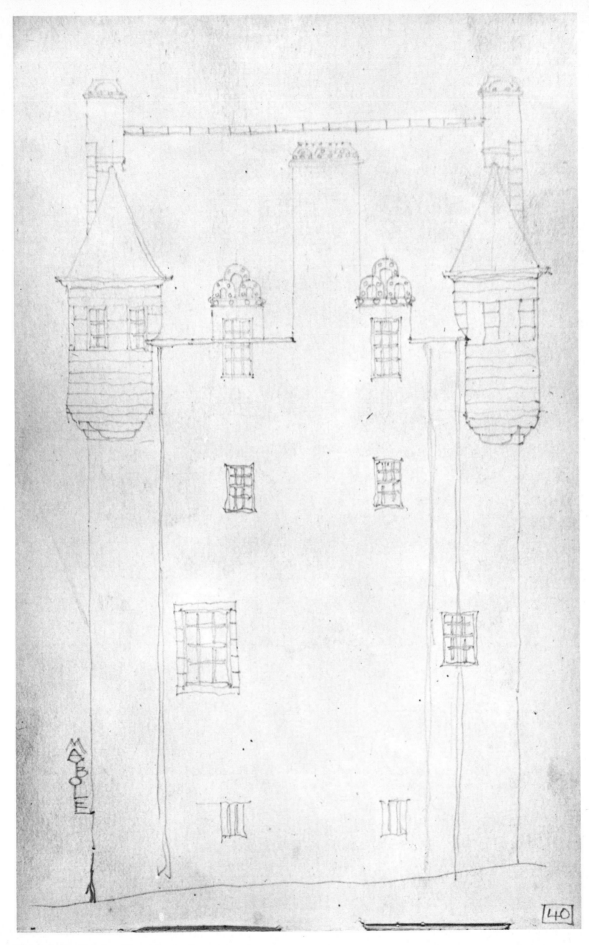

Maybole Castle, Ayrshire, 1895 176 × 115 GU

43

The Fossil Depot, Lyme Regis, 1895 260 × 205 GU
Mackintosh made several studies at Lyme Regis in 1895, usually
of small houses, the bay windows of which were the source for the
windows in the central bay of the Glasgow School of Art. Some of
these Dorset sketches were illustrated in the *British Architect*,
XLIV, 1895, pp 332–3 and 388–9.

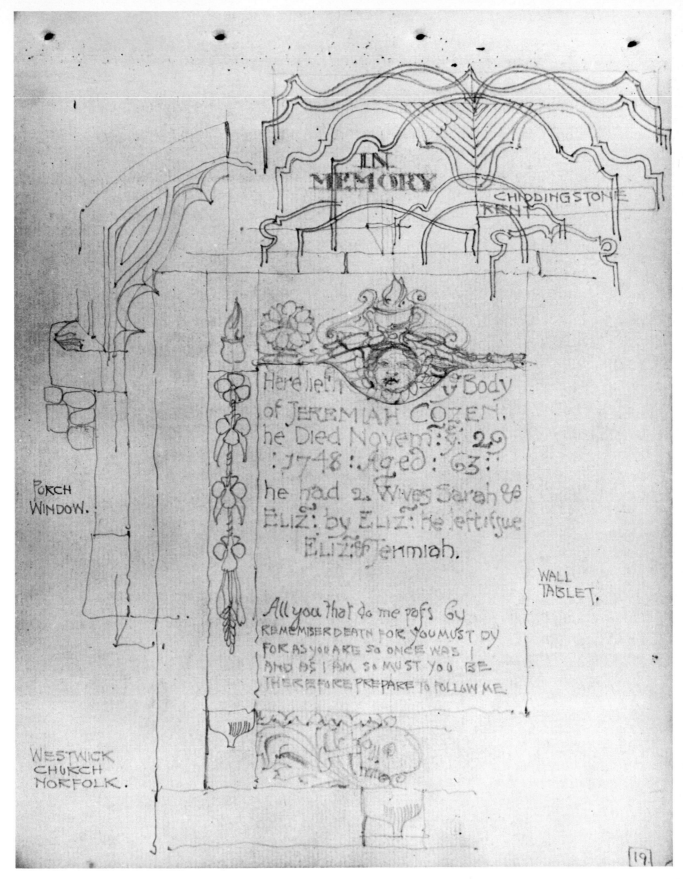

Memorial wall tablet, Westwick Church, Norfolk, 1897 228 × 180
In this drawing Mackintosh has combined details of a window in
the church with a wall tablet. He took the same sketchbook with
him to Chiddingstone in 1910, and other details of gravestone
carving are overlaid on the earlier drawing. (See page 89.)

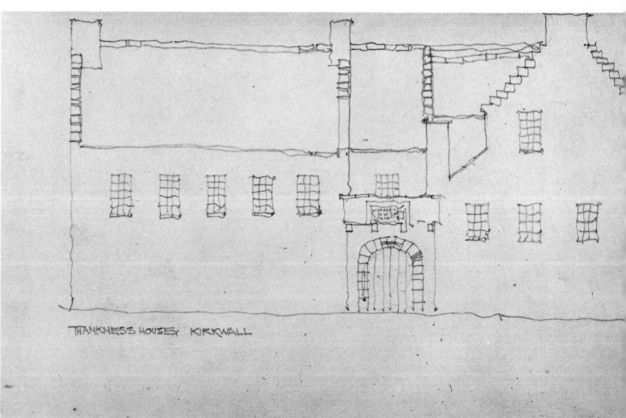

THANKNESS HOUSES, KIRKWALL

House, Worstead, 1897 134 × 370 GU
Although Mackintosh dates this drawing *1896* it seems likely that
this was a mistake, as Worstead is in the same area he visited in
August, 1897; no other drawings of East Anglia dated 1896 are
known.

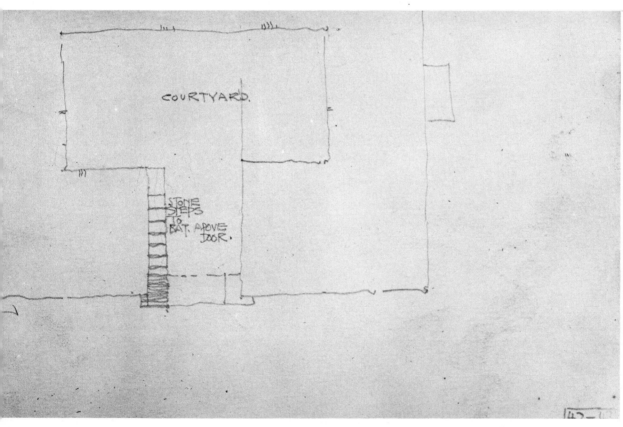

Thankness House, Kirkwall, Orkney, c.1896–9 115 × 352 GU
Mackintosh's travels around Scotland are not as well documented as his English visits, and no dated drawings of this visit are now known. Stylistically it can be dated to the later half of the 1890s, but it would be intriguing to date it post-1898, when Mackintosh could have seen Melsetter House, Hoy, designed by W. R. Lethaby, who had so greatly inspired him in the early 1890s.

MERRIOT CHURCH
SOMERSETSHIRE

Merriott Church, Somerset, 1895 362 ×
127 GU
This church tower is undoubtedly the
inspiration for the tower of Queens
Cross Church, Glasgow, 1897, the
battering of the tower and the inset
polygonal turret being major features of
both buildings. Mackintosh also used
the inset polygonal tower on the east
front of the School of Art, although
here it is used as an oriel, supported on
a huge stone corbel.

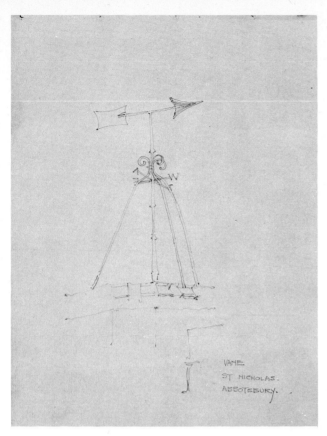

Weather vane, St. Nicholas, Abbotsbury, 1895 260 × 205 GU

Details of capitals, Whitchurch Canonicorum, 1895
260 × 205 GU

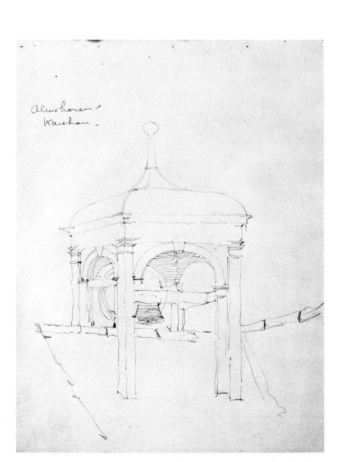

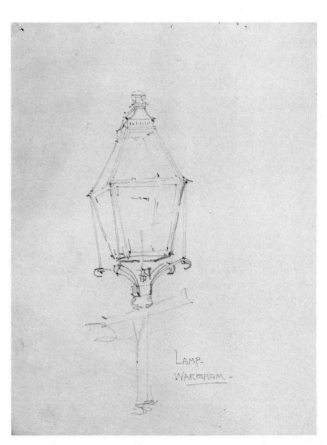

Bell turret, Almshouse, Wareham, 1895 260 × 205 GU

Lamp, Wareham, 1895 260 × 205 GU

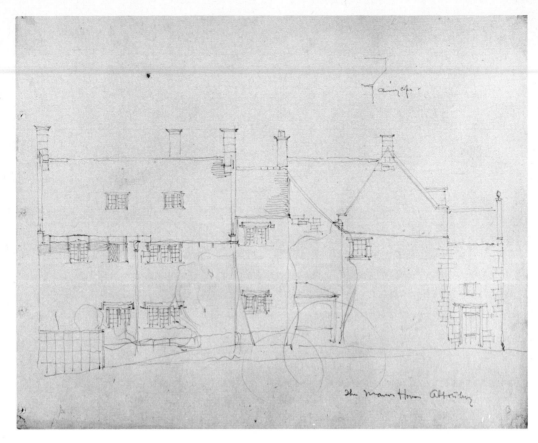

The Manor House, Abbotsbury, 1895 205 × 260 GU

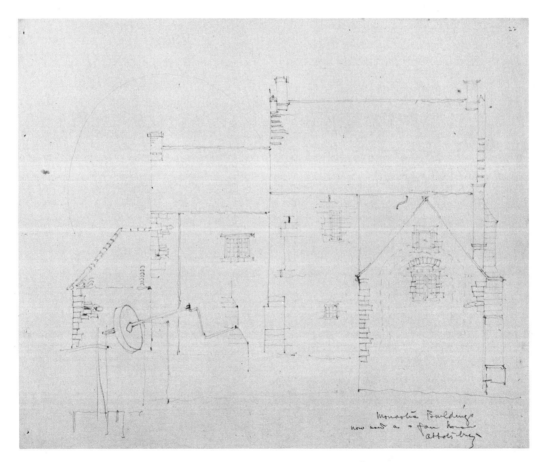

Farmhouse, previously monastic buildings, Abbotsbury, 1895 205 × 260 GU

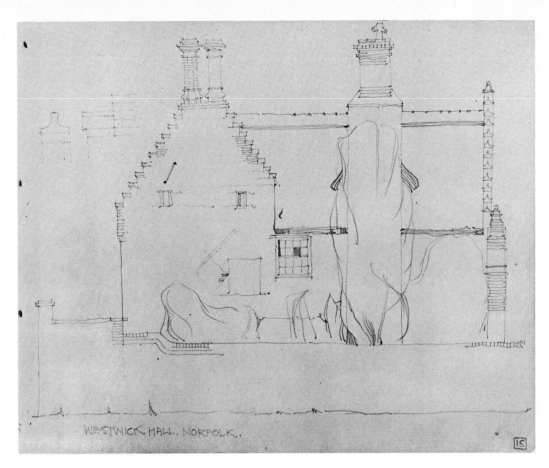

Westwick Hall, Norfolk, 1897 180 × 228 GU

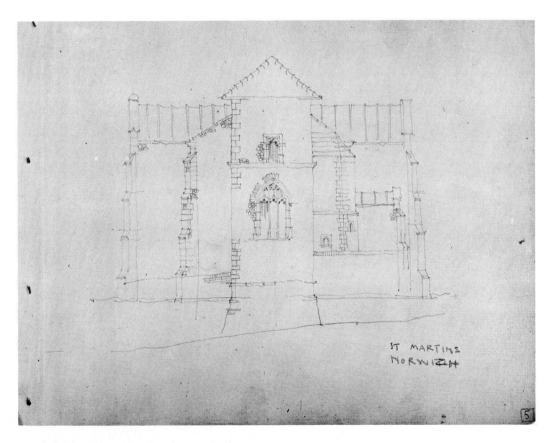

St. Martin's Church, Norwich, 1897 180 × 228 GU

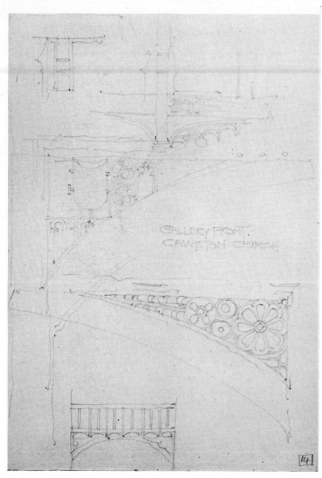

Details of carved gallery spandrels, Cawston Church, 1897
185 × 134 GU

Carved screen panels, Swanton Abbot Church, 1897 228 × 180 GU

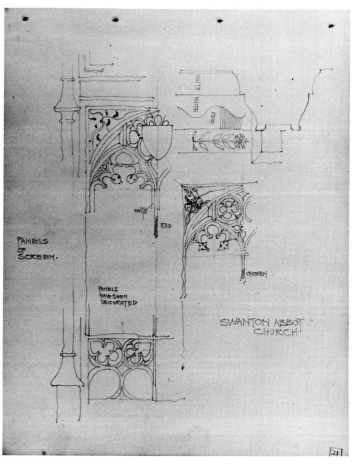

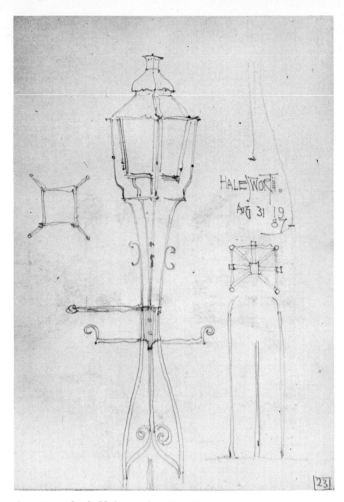

Lamp standard, Halesworth, 1897 185 × 134 GU

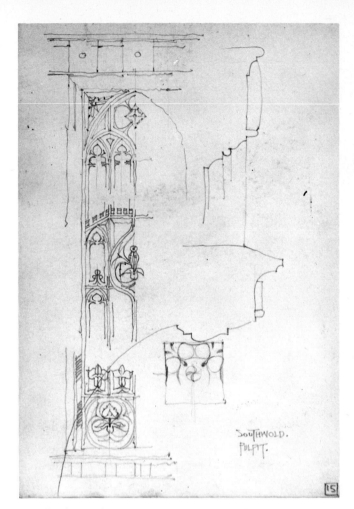

Details of the pulpit, Southwold Church, Suffolk, 1897
185 × 134 GU

Rain water head, handles and other details, Tavistock, Devon, 1898
185 × 134 GU

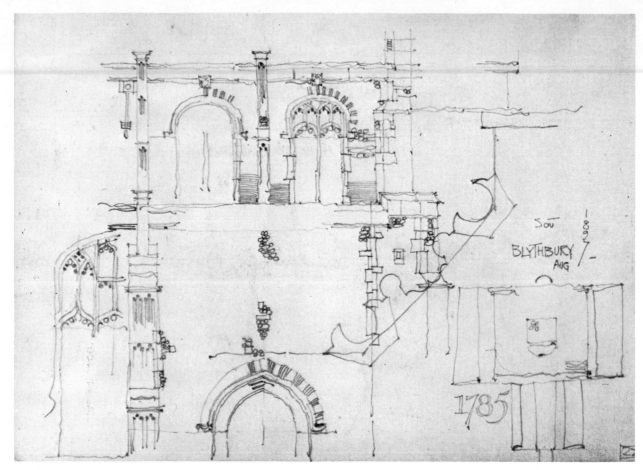

Details, Blythbury Church, 1897 134 × 185 GU

East Elevation, Blythbury Church, 1897 185 × 134 GU

Blackthorn, Chiddingstone, 1910 258 × 202 GU

Cuckoo flower, Chiddingstone, 1910 258 × 202 GU

Larkspur, Walberswick, 1914 258 × 202 GU

Fritillaria, Walberswick, 1915 251 × 202 GU
The chequered motif had been a favourite device of Mackintosh
in his interior decorations from about 1901 onwards. This flower
must have had a special appeal for him, and he deliberately repeats
the pattern of the flower in black and white in the signature panel.

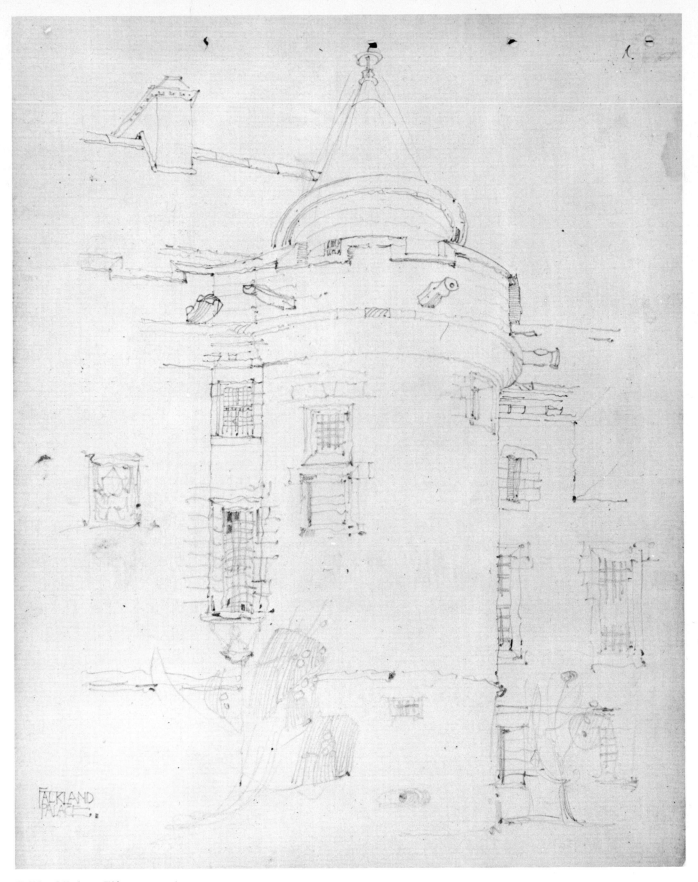

Falkland Palace, Fife, c.1900 260 × 203 GU

Framlingham Castle, 1897 370 × 134 GU
The handling of this subject, with the flowers in
the foreground, looks forward to the Holy Island
drawings of 1901 (Frontispiece and pp 68, 69,
70, 71).

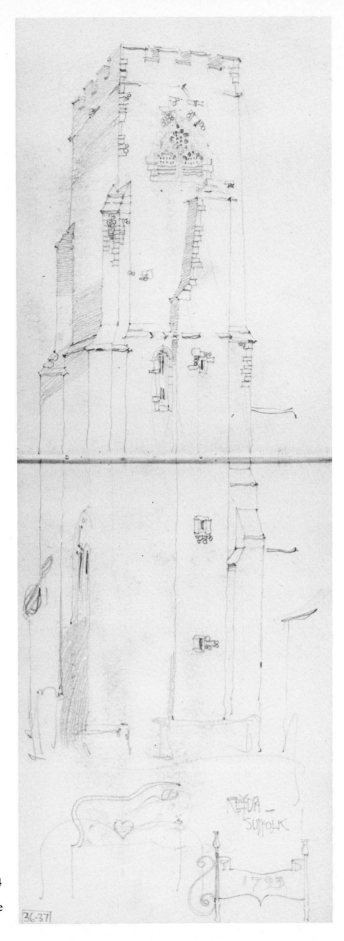

Church Tower, Reydon, Suffolk, 1897 370 × 134
GU
Mackintosh uses up the undrawn area of his page
to record more tombstone details.

61

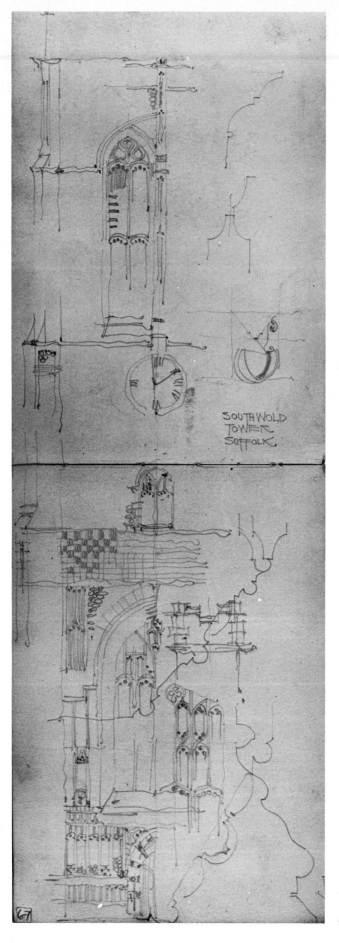

SOUTHWOLD
TOWER
SUFFOLK.

Church tower, Southwold, Suffolk, 1897 370 × 134 GU

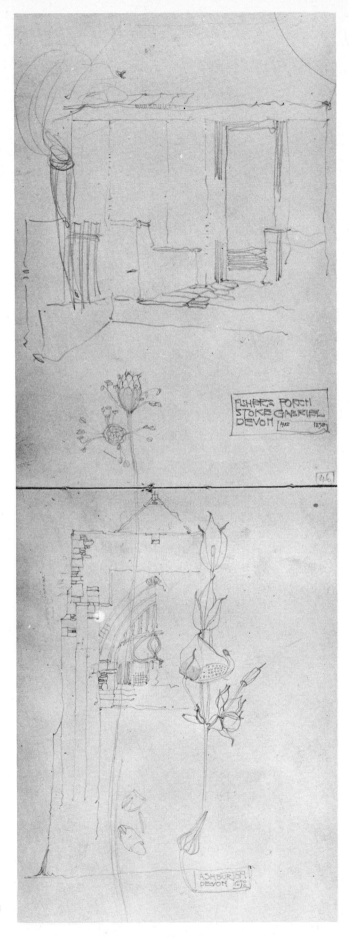

*Fisherman's porch, Stoke Gabriel and details of a
church, Ashburton, Devon, 1898* 370 × 134 GU

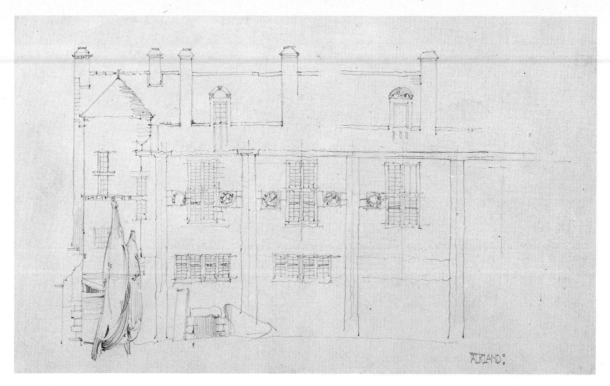

Falkland Palace, Fife, c.1900 203 × 260 GU

There is no record of Mackintosh's visit to Falkland Palace, but on stylistic grounds a date of around 1900 is suggested. The lack of the joint initials CRM & MMM implies that the drawing was made before his marriage in August, 1900. According to Howarth (p. 181) Mackintosh had a job in Fife about 1900, at St. Serf's Church, Dysart, not too far from Falkland, and these drawings were possibly made on one of his visits to Dysart. In 1904, when designing Scotland Street School, Mackintosh must have referred to these drawings, for the range of windows between two round towers is too close to be just a coincidence. On some of the early drawings for the school, apparently worked out by an assistant, the resemblance is even closer, even repeating the band of carved decoration on the tower which is also visible in this drawing.

Outhouses, Saxlingham, 1905 203 × 260 GU

The superimposed drawing of a bolt becomes a surrealist addition to the building.

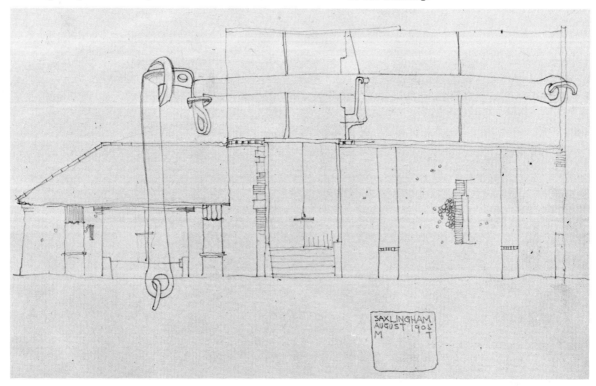

St. Cuthbert's Church, Holy Island, 1901 203 × 260 GU
The way in which the flower has been superimposed on a different
scale over the church recalls the Ashburton drawing of 1898 (p. 63).
M is Margaret, T is Toshie, Mackintosh's nickname.

St. Cuthbert's Church, Holy Island, 1901 203 × 260 GU

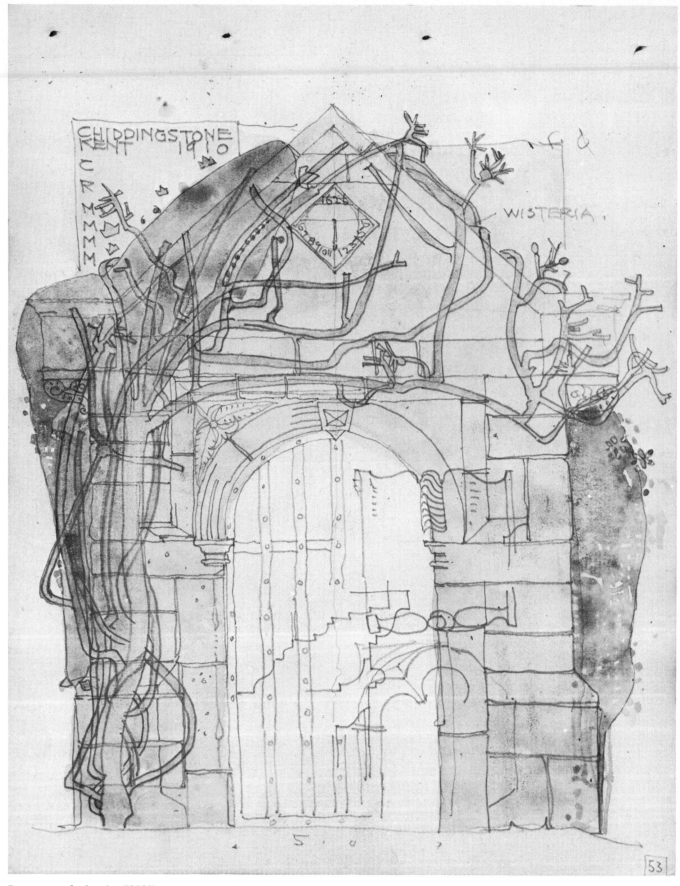

Doorway and wisteria, Chiddingstone, 1910 228 × 180 GU

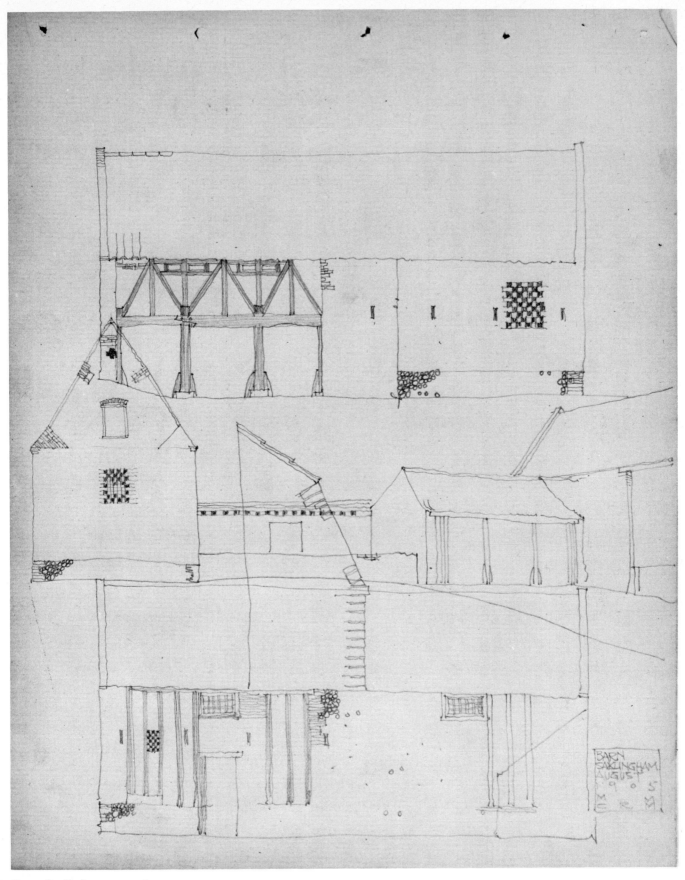

Barn, Saxlingham, 1905 260 × 203 GU

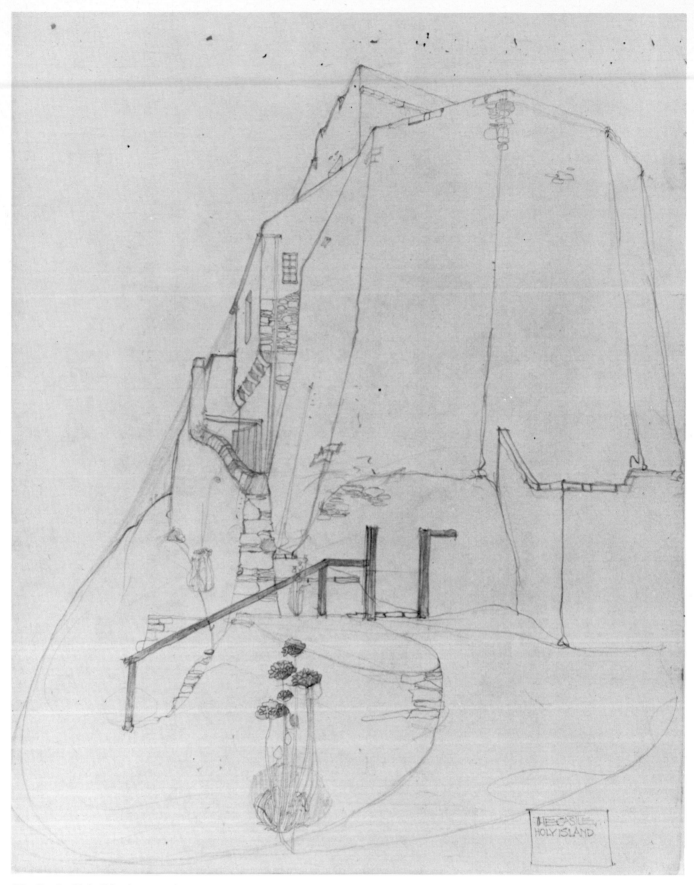

The Castle, Holy Island, 1901 260 × 203 GU

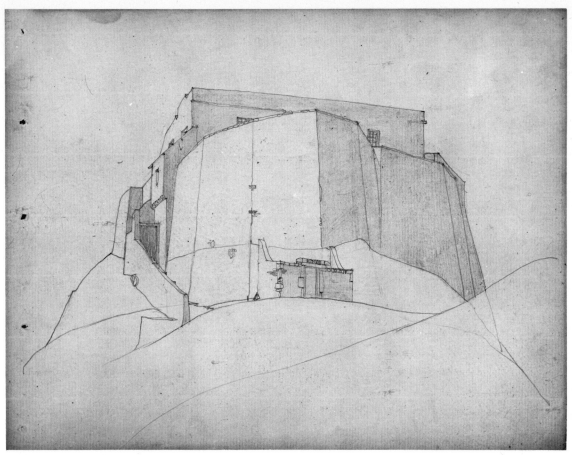

The Castle, Holy Island, 1901 203 × 260 GU

The Castle, Holy Island, 1901 203 × 260 GU

Previous page

TOP
The Castle, Holy Island, 1901 203 × 260 GU
Howarth (p. 43) states that the Mackintoshes spent their honey-
moon on Holy Island, but if this was taken immediately after their
wedding in August 1900, then no drawings have survived (if,
indeed, any were made). Holy Island obviously became a favourite
resort of the Mackintoshes, and they were joined there in 1901 by
Herbert and Frances MacNair and Charles Macdonald; in 1906
they visited it again (see p. 73).

BOTTOM
The Castle, Holy Island, 1901 203 × 260 GU
It is about this time that Mackintosh began to incorporate both
his own and Margaret's initials on a drawing (see Introduction
p. 9). The clumps of sea pinks were to have a whole page of his
book devoted to them (see p. 38).

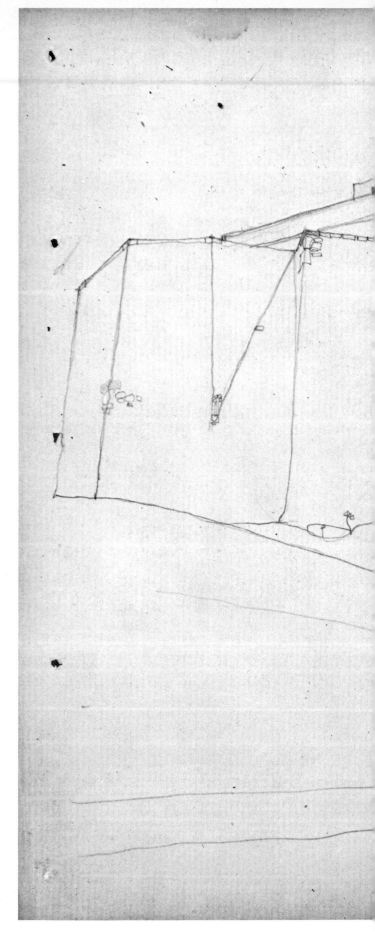

The Castle, Holy Island, 203 × 260 GU
The relationship between this view of the castle and the south
elevation of the Glasgow School of Art tempts one to believe that
Mackintosh must have known it before the designs for the School
were made in 1897.

THE CASTLE
HOLY ISLAND
JULY 1901

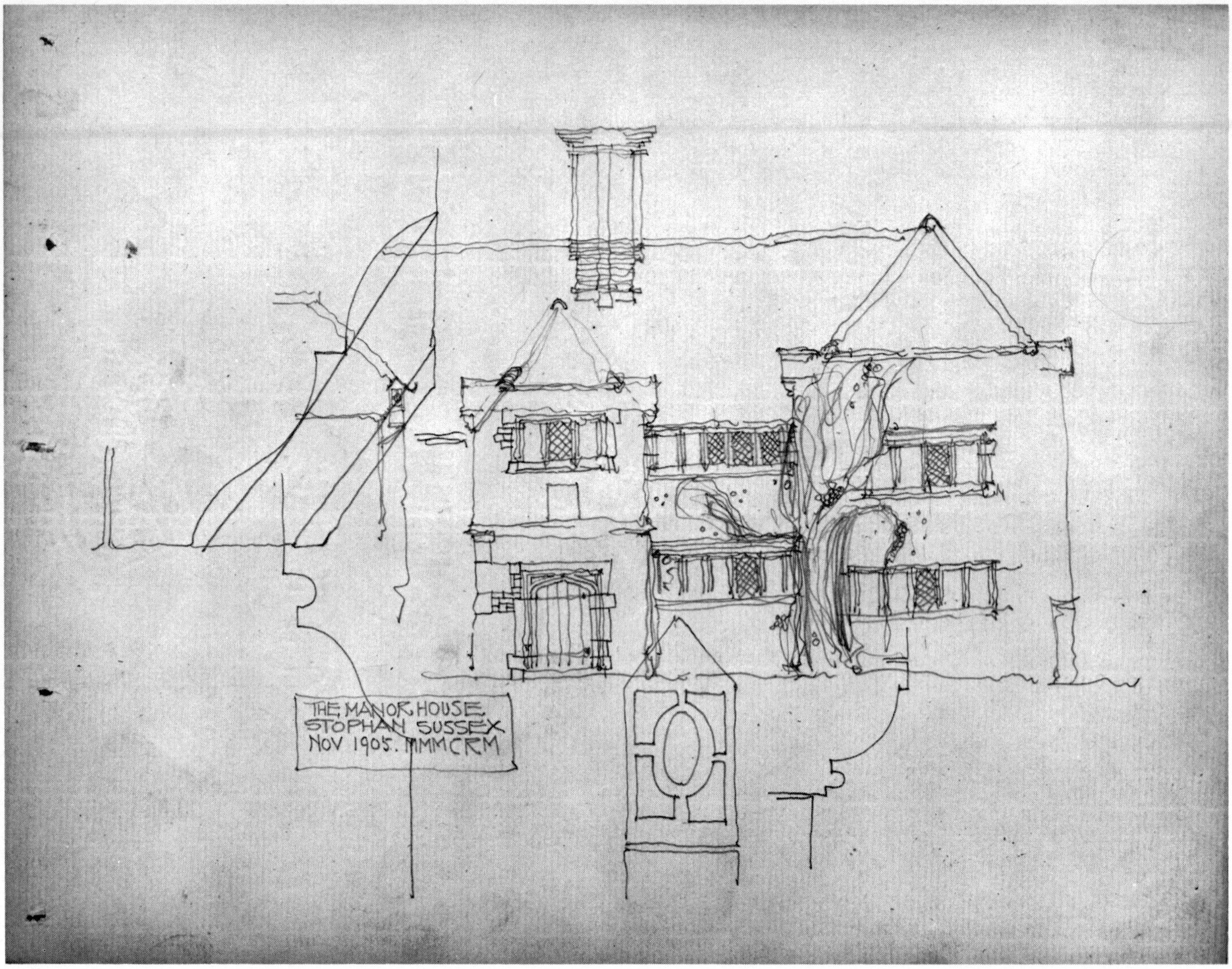

The Manor House, Stopham, Sussex, 1905 203 × 260 GU

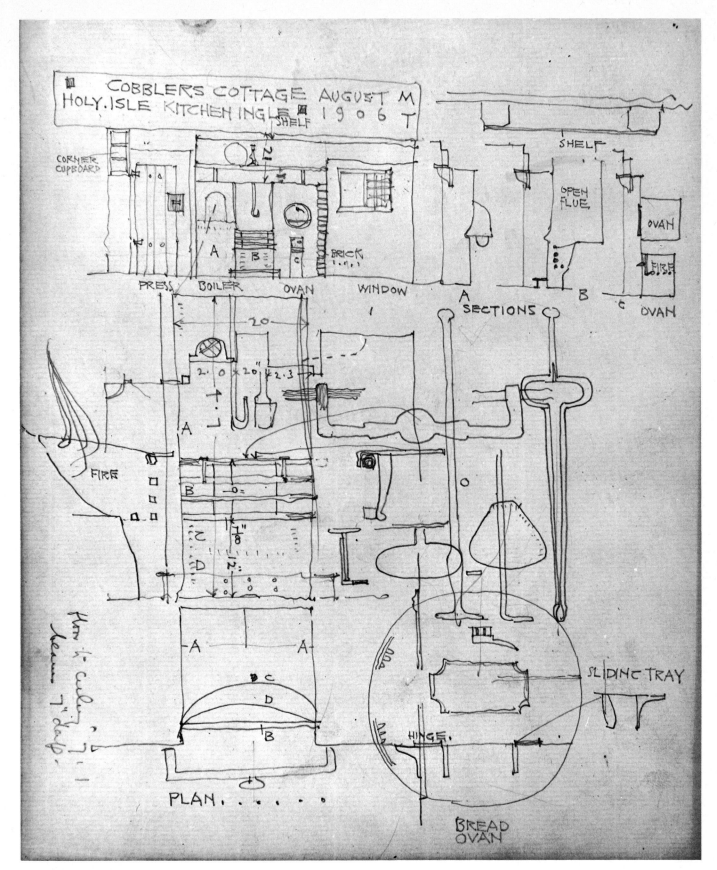

Cobbler's Cottage, Holy Island, 1906 260 × 203 GU
The fireplaces in Mackintosh's own buildings were usually based
on traditional designs like this. Here he has tried to record as much
information as possible about the construction, with sections,
plans and details carefully laid out on the page, alongside drawings
of the fire irons, oven trays and handles.

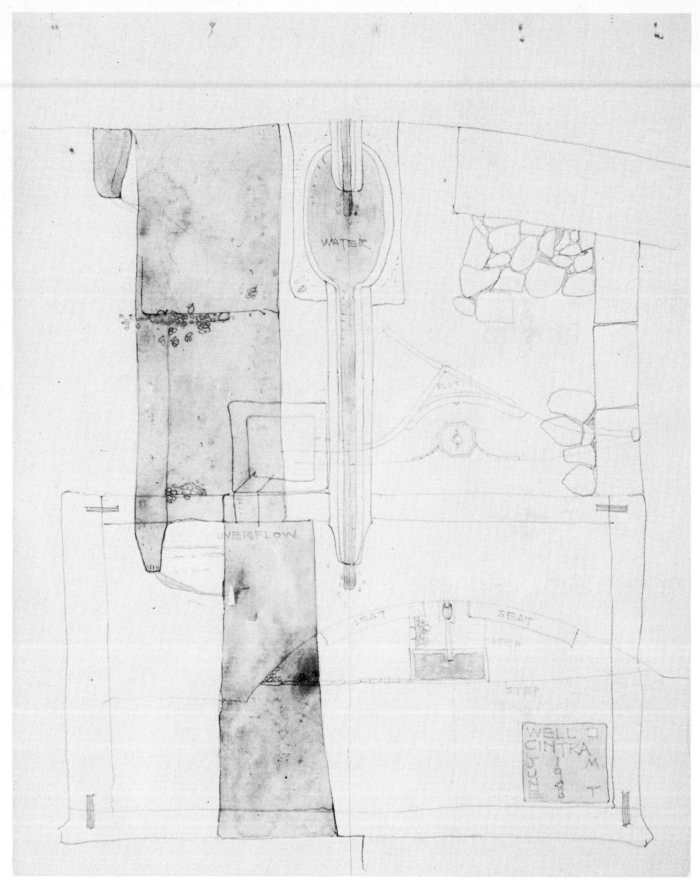

Well, Cintra, Portugal, 1908 260 × 203 GU
Mackintosh here records a site plan, a detail plan and sections all
on one sheet, making an overall decorative pattern. Turn the page
on its side to see the section, which is detailed in watercolour.

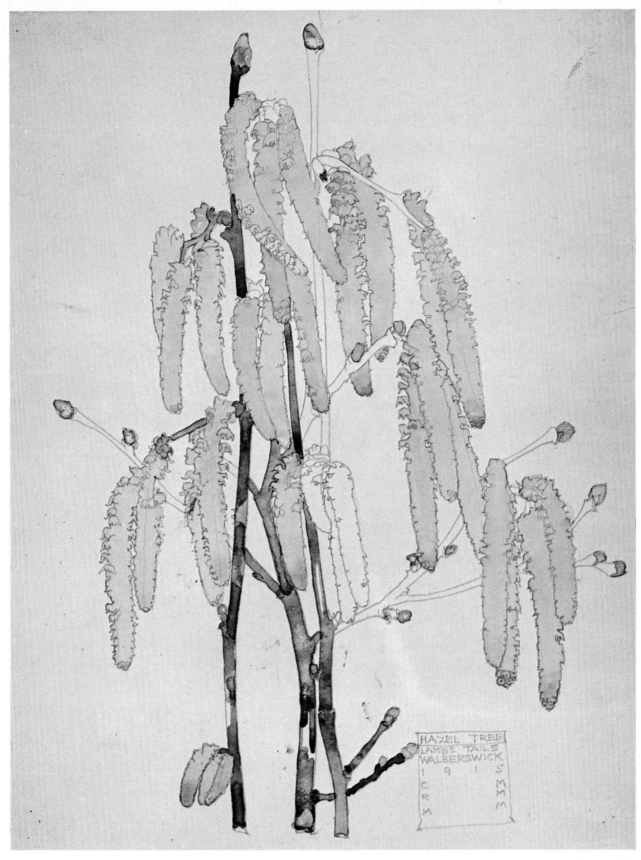

Hazel tree, lambs' tails, Walberswick, 1915 280 × 207 GU

Japanese witch hazel, Walberswick, 1915 263 × 211 GU
Mackintosh's spelling falters again – the only criticism that can
be made of an otherwise perfect drawing.

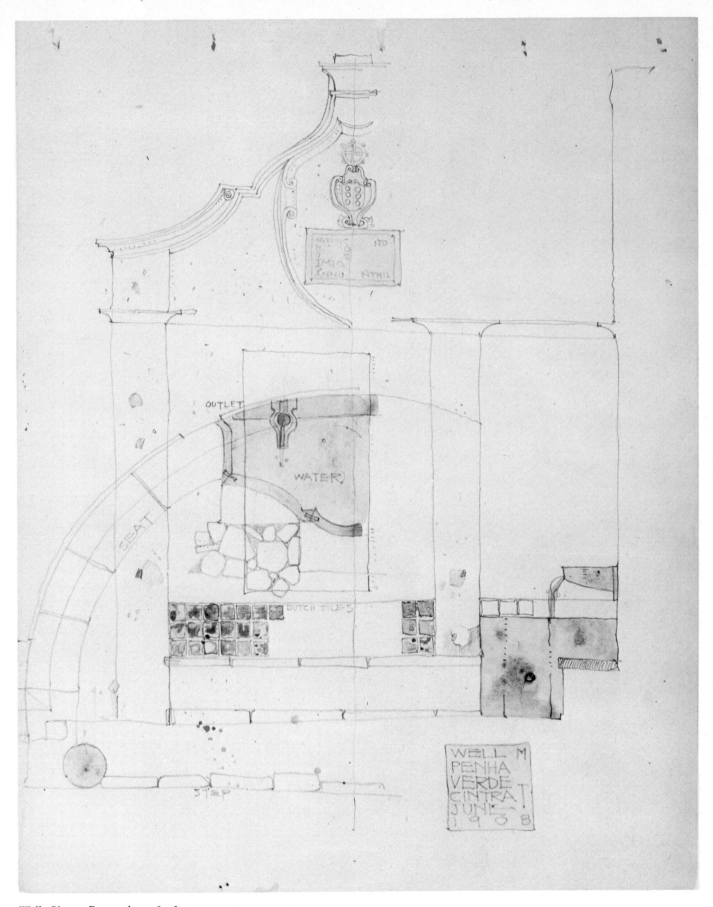

Well, Cintra, Portugal, 1908 260 × 203 GU

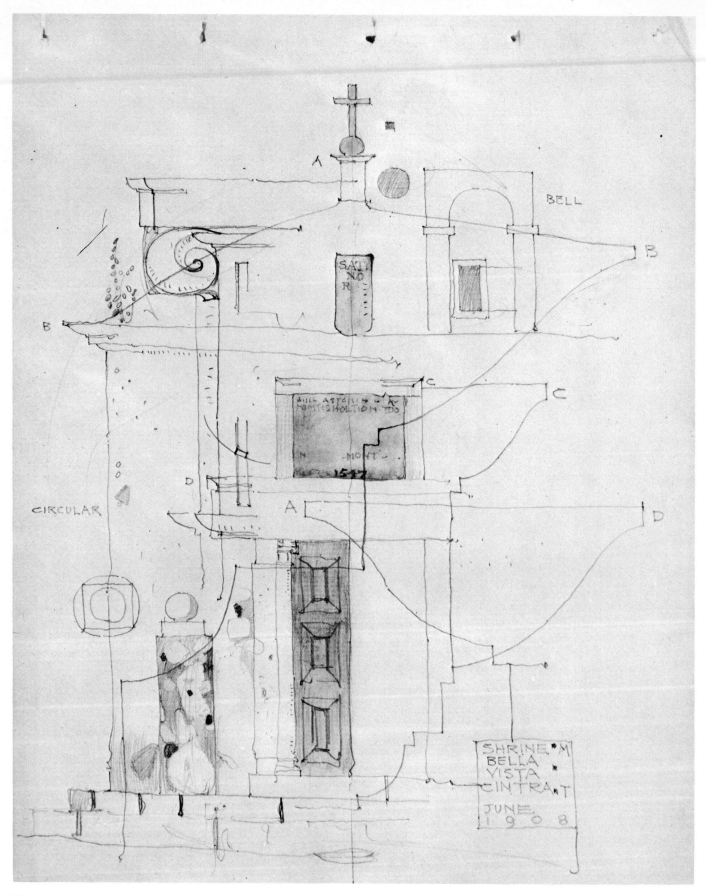

Shrine, Cintra, Portugal, 1908 260 × 203 GU

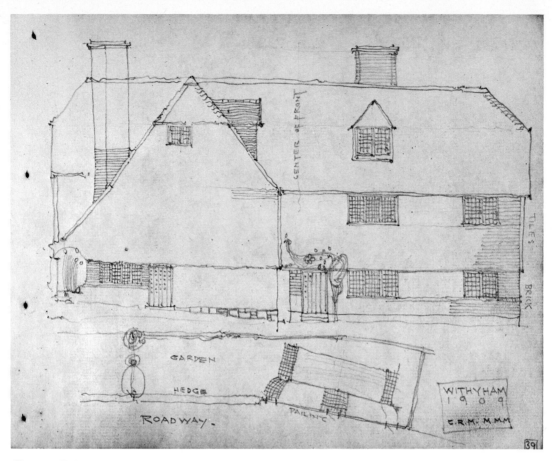

House at Withyham, Sussex, 1909 180 × 228 GU

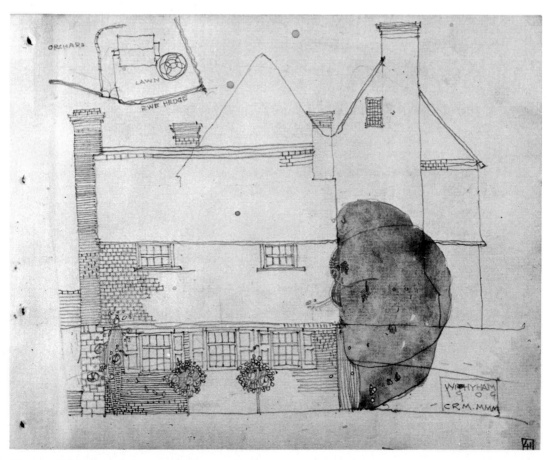

House at Withyham, Sussex, 1909 180 × 228 GU

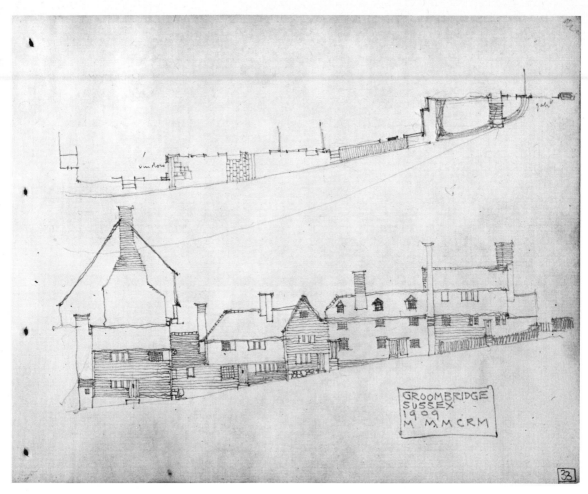

GROOMBRIDGE
SUSSEX
1909
M MCRM

GROOMBRIDGE
SUSSEX
1909

The Dorset Arms, Withyham, Sussex, 1909 180 × 228 GU
The change of style apparent in the Holy Island drawings of 1901
is confirmed in these Sussex drawings. The subjects are chosen
as much for the picturesque qualities as anything else, and the
drawings are far more decorative than the sketches of the 1890s.

Opposite

TOP
Plan and elevation of a Street at Groombridge, Sussex, 1909
180 × 228 GU
In the same sketchbook is an undated drawing proposing a new
layout for the village of Killearn, near Glasgow; Mackintosh was
possibly collecting information for that project. Quite close to
Groombridge are two houses by R. Norman Shaw, Glen Aldred
and Leys Wood which Mackintosh might have seen while on his
tour of the south-east.

BOTTOM
House at Groombridge, Sussex, 1909 180 × 228 GU

Newton Castle, Blairgowrie, Perthshire, 1909 228 × 180 GU

House, Walberswick, Suffolk, 1914 180 × 228 GU
This sketch appears to be the last in the style Mackintosh developed between 1891 and 1910, and is one of the few non-botanical drawings of Walberswick. After 1914, Mackintosh concentrated his artistic output into flower drawings, and highly-finished watercolours.

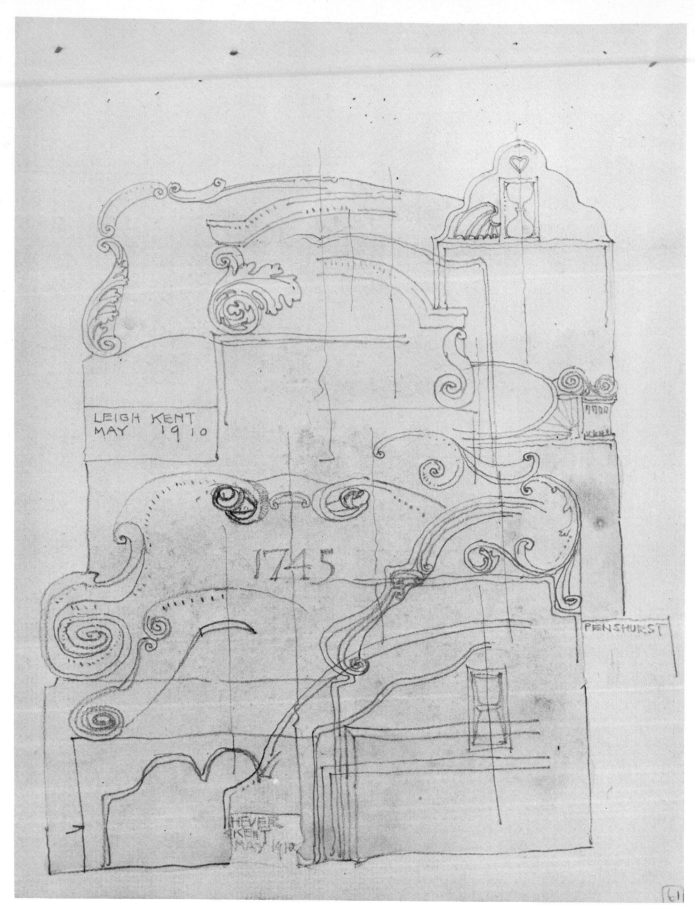

Gravestones, Hever, Leigh and Penshurst, Kent, 1910 228 × 180 GU
Details from three churchyards have been grouped together, on
one sheet, and given an overall decorative coherence by the
application of a thin colour wash.

Willow herb, Buxted, 1919 258 × 200 GU
Mackintosh did some work at East Grinstead in this year, and in
1920 he had a small commission at Burgess Hill, both of which are
near Buxted in Sussex.

Mimosa, Amélie-les-Bains, 1924 257 × 210 GU

From 1923, after giving up architecture completely, Mackintosh began to spend a great deal of time in France. There he began a series of highly-finished watercolours, on a much larger scale than these sketches of flowers. His intention was to begin another career as an artist, and the quality of these new works would have confirmed his hopes. Sadly, he died before being able to complete enough pictures for an exhibition in London.

Petunia, Walberswick, 1914 258 × 202 GU

Mackintosh appears to have left Glasgow in the early summer of 1914, and he and his wife went to stay in Walberswick. There he produced a series of flower drawings, and a number of water-colour studies of the surrounding landscape, developing the themes and style of his Sussex and Kent drawings of 1909 and 1910.

Jasmine, Walberswick, 1915 276 × 209 GU

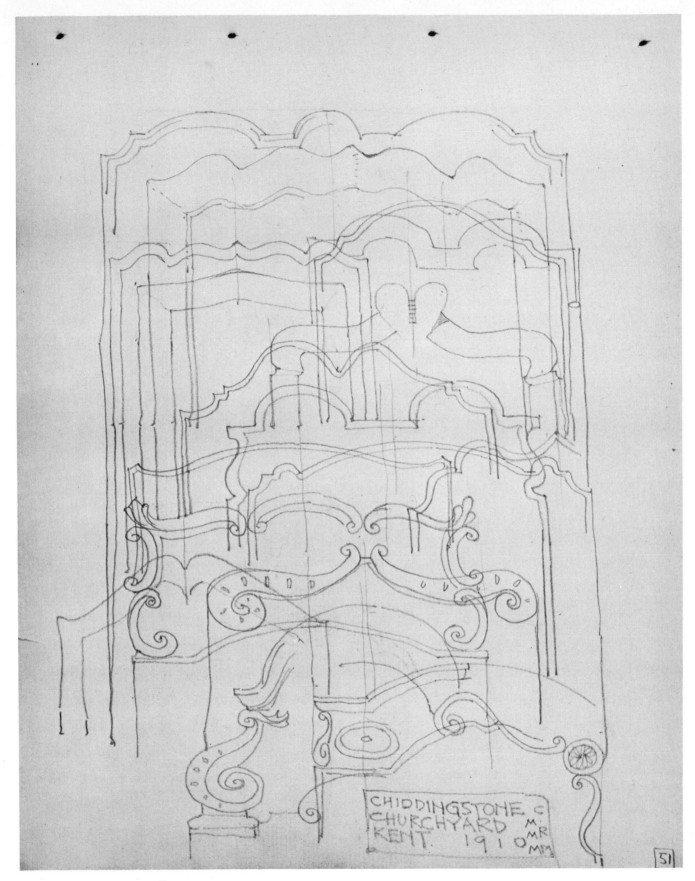

Gravestones, Chiddingstone, Kent, 1910 228 × 180 GU

Cottage, Chiddingstone, Kent, 1910 180 × 228 GU

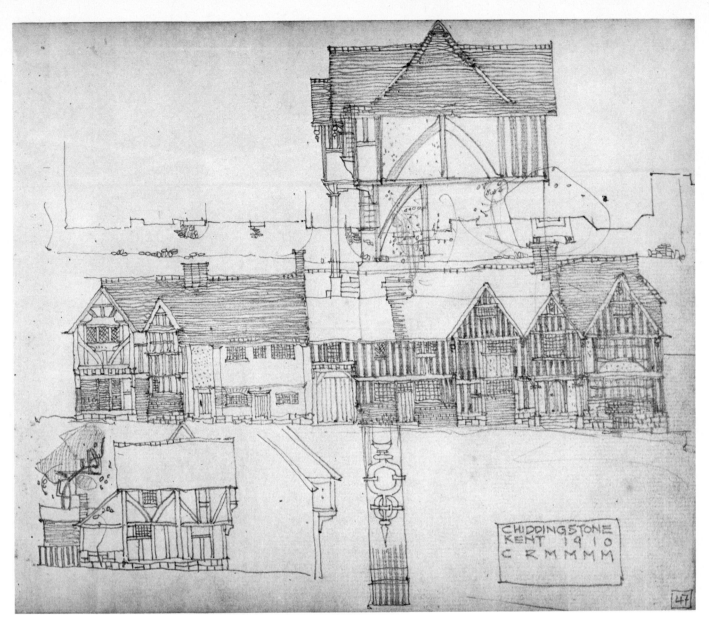

Houses, Chiddingstone, Kent, 1910 180 × 228 GU
Once again, Mackintosh has combined plan, section, detail and
side and front elevations for artistic effect.

CHIDDINGSTONE KENT

Houses, Chiddingstone, Kent, 1910 180 × 228 GU
A larger scale sketch of some of the houses on p. 91.

Houses, Chiddingstone, Kent, 1910 180 × 228 GU

Oasthouses, Chiddingstone, Kent, 1910 180 × 228 GU

Oasthouses, Chiddingstone, Kent, 1910 180 × 228 GU

The Dower House, Chiddingstone, Kent, 1910 180 × 228 GU